THE
ALTERNATIVE

AWAKEN YOUR DREAM,

UNITE YOUR COMMUNITY,

AND LIVE IN HOPE

THE
ALTERNATIVE

BY CALEB STANLEY & AUSTIN DENNIS

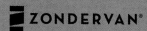

ZONDERVAN

The Alternative
Copyright © 2019 by Caleb Stanley and Austin Dennis

Requests for information should be addressed to:
Zondervan, *3900 Sparks Dr. SE, Grand Rapids, Michigan 49546*

ISBN 978-0-310-76588-2 (softcover)

ISBN 978-0-310-76586-8 (ebook)

Published in association with Books & Such Literary Management, 52 Mission Circle, Suite 122, PMB 170, Santa Rosa, California 95409-5370, www.booksandsuch.com.

Wedding photo on page 158 copyright Michelle Taulbee, Michelle Taulbee Photography

Cover design: Ron Huizinga
Interior design: Denise Froehlich

Printed in China

18 19 20 21 22 23 / DSC / 10 9 8 7 6 5 4 3 2 1

This book is dedicated to my grandfather, Allan,
who showed me what it means to leave a legacy.
—Caleb

I want to dedicate this book to my wife and daughter: Thank you for constantly pushing me to accomplish more than I ever thought I could, and for allowing me to chase the dream God put in my heart years ago. Without your love and support, I would not be where I am today. And to my mom and dad: Thank you for providing a foundation for me to walk on where I could chase after the calling God set on my life at a young age. Thank you for guiding me in my young years and showing grace in moments when I didn't deserve it, and for teaching me to "Fear no man, ONLY GOD."

—Austin

CONTENTS

THE ALTERNATIVE IS MORE THAN AN EVENT—IT'S A LIFESTYLE. IT'S ABOUT CHOOSING HOPE WHEN LIFE HAS BROKEN YOU. IT'S DECIDING TO DREAM AGAIN WHEN YOU'VE BEEN LET DOWN. IT'S THE ALTERNATIVE TO THE EMPTINESS AND BROKENNESS WE ALL FACE. IT'S FINDING JESUS ON THE JOURNEY.

THEALTERNATIVE.ORG

FOREWORD

BY JOHN LUKE ROBERTSON

If you're anything like me, you want God to use your life in big ways. But it can sometimes feel like those dreams and desires are hard to hold on to. We've all been in seasons where we don't feel like we are really making a difference. At times, we wonder how God could ever use us … or if God can ever forgive something in our past, or a mistake we've recently made. Some of you who are about to read this book may even be going through seasons of great pain and confusion. Maybe you have lost someone you love, and the world feels dark. Maybe you are simply trying to figure out what God's plan *is* for your life. No matter what we face, the confusion and doubts we experience in life can feel overwhelming when we start to focus on all the things that seem to stand in the way of our callings. The good news is, there is an alternative.

Caleb and Austin have spent the last several years reaching people with a message that God wants to use their lives, no matter the season they are in or what they've experienced. The message of The Alternative has reminded me and thousands of others that we don't have to settle for what the world offers. Our pain and our suffering are temporary. There is more beyond the discouragement and disappointment of our world. When we put our faith in Jesus, our lives can take a radical turn. We can take big steps. We can dream big dreams. We can watch God use our lives when we give them to Him! From the behind-the-scenes view of event planning to the letdown of failed attempts, even the prayers and personal struggles shared in this book, I believe Caleb and Austin's vulnerability will inspire you to action. We've all been given a dream, and it's my prayer that the way these guys have pursued The Alternative will challenge you to take a deep look at what God has placed in your heart and called you to do.

Don't settle for the status quo. Don't stop short of your calling. Take the path of greatest resistance. Awaken your dream, unite your community, and live in hope.

Find The Alternative.

John Luke

INTRODUCTION

CALEB

I'll never forget watching my pen try to keep up with the thoughts pouring from my mind. It was 3:50 in the morning. Waking up in the middle of the night was not my usual habit, but there I was on that April morning in 2016, wide awake and spilling ink onto the page. Restlessness and discontent had settled over me, and I couldn't quiet those feelings. I had heard messages about people battling depression and anxiety—could that be what I was experiencing?

But, no, this felt different. I couldn't be depressed. From where I sat, everything in my life was going great. I should have been happy. I was twenty-two years old and helping pastor a young church on the south side of Atlanta alongside some of my best friends. I was comfortable. I was preaching and getting to travel. I was making enough money to live on my own, while still saving for the future. Home was a beautiful loft overlooking the small town of Hogansville, Georgia. My friends had just purchased the loft next door to turn it into a creative community for filmmakers and entrepreneurs. My girlfriend at the time was acting in some pretty big films, and I was flying to LA every couple of weeks to spend time with her. Not only was my personal life great, our church vision was growing.

Everything seemed perfect.

So why was I feeling so much unrest? When life is perfect, you're not supposed to feel like . . . this.

Maybe I should make some changes?

Nope, that doesn't seem right . . . I wouldn't change anything about life right now.

But then what's my problem?

It was like God woke me up in the middle of the night to have an argument with myself. There were so many things in my heart that I had been dismissing, dreams of greater things. I thought the root of these desires was discontent, and I was trained to think that being discontent was a sin. But God was using my discontent to push me toward something.

I just didn't know *what*.

That night, my soul felt like it was caught in a rip current, and I didn't know how to break free. So I started writing, hoping it would help me understand everything I was feeling.

What if we do something big in our old hometown? What if we get the old team together? Our community needs it. What if we dream again?

As I wrote, something inside me began to change. What started in my journal had migrated onto the glass coffee table (which I'd made from an old sheet of glass and some cinder blocks). I was draining the life from an Expo marker as I scribbled out questions I normally would have dismissed.

Was I living the life God wanted for me? Was I judging the quality of my life against those around me or against my calling?

I asked God what He wanted me to change. I even whispered to Him, "If I wanted to make these changes . . . how? How could I possibly? Where would I even start?" I believe God is trying to awaken something in all of us. Whether a dream or a calling, it's time for us to listen.

I went back to bed that night and told God that if He wanted me to change something, He would need to make it obvious.

He did.

AUSTIN

I was standing at a Kroger gas pump, preparing to head back to my office after lunch break. It was January 27, 2016, and my life was about to change forever.

My wife, Rachel, and I had moved to the small town of LaGrange, Georgia, in September 2015. LaGrange was about an hour south of Newnan, where I had grown up. I'd moved down there to take a youth pastor position at a church that was thriving.

By all accounts, God had blessed me. I had a great job with a good income for a twenty-three-year-old. My wife and I had been married for two months, and we had our own house. I was living the life.

That January day, I'd had a great lunch with my wife. We'd tried a new place in town—it was all right, nothing special—but the conversation was good. We had dreamed about where God would lead us over the next five years. The future was wide open.

As we were leaving the restaurant, Rachel made a comment: "I don't feel too well."

This launched a thousand questions from me: "Are you okay? Are you sick? Do you have the flu? Are you dying?" I sounded like my mom.

After I settled down, Rachel asked if I would take her to the local Walgreens and then drop her back off at work. I agreed, thinking she was going to grab some Tylenol or Advil. But as she walked out of Walgreens, I could see the small box through her bag: a pregnancy test.

Um . . . what?

Yes, it was a pregnancy test. Rachel said she was running late and she would have to get back to work before she could take it. We would have to wait a while for the results.

Then, as I stood at that gas pump, a text came through from my wife.

It was a picture—of a positive pregnancy test.

I released the gas pump and stared at my phone. I was going to be a dad.

You're too young. You don't have it all together. You don't have enough money. You're not ready. Not ready, not ready, not ready!

We panicked at first. But as the months went by, Rachel and I watched the pregnancy unfold. We were thrilled. We were going to be *parents*.

We matured quickly. Before long, we were going to have another life to care for. The responsibility weighed heavily on our thoughts. Our discussions of the future shifted dramatically. It was no longer, "Where do you want to travel?" It was, "How will we raise our little girl?"

We wanted to be parents who would live and lead by faith. That is easier said than done.

Four days after Esther Rose was born, I sat down with my head pastor and told him I was stepping away from my youth pastor position. You might be saying to yourself, "I thought you were going to be responsible. You quit your job with a newborn at home? Who does that?!"

I had to. God had placed a dream to start a ministry in my heart back in 2010, and I knew I hadn't fully embraced it. The weight of that dream had become too heavy to ignore. Even though it made no sense, I was about to make massive changes to my life—just when I should have been clinging to stability.

So, the day after Christmas, we packed our bags and left town, determined to follow our hearts. But were we ready for what God had in store?

TIMELINE OF THE ALTERNATIVE

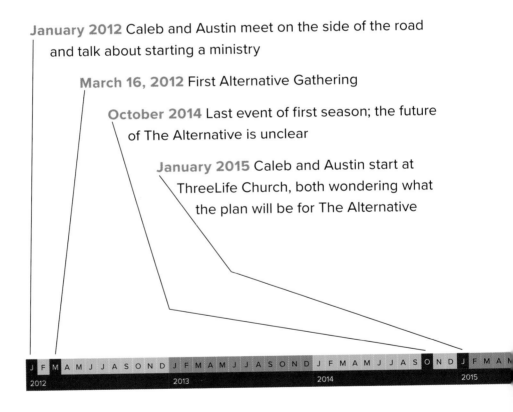

January 2012 Caleb and Austin meet on the side of the road and talk about starting a ministry

March 16, 2012 First Alternative Gathering

October 2014 Last event of first season; the future of The Alternative is unclear

January 2015 Caleb and Austin start at ThreeLife Church, both wondering what the plan will be for The Alternative

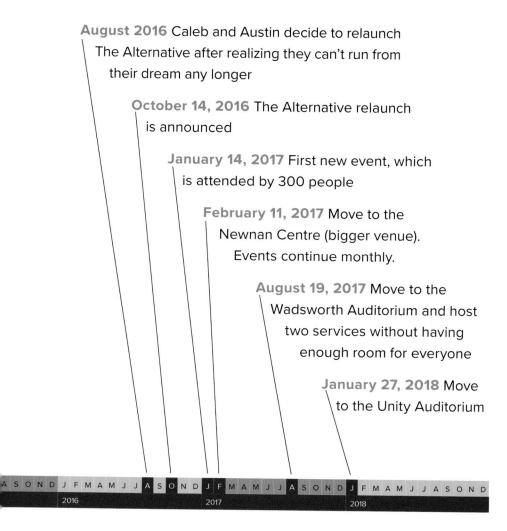

August 2016 Caleb and Austin decide to relaunch The Alternative after realizing they can't run from their dream any longer

October 14, 2016 The Alternative relaunch is announced

January 14, 2017 First new event, which is attended by 300 people

February 11, 2017 Move to the Newnan Centre (bigger venue). Events continue monthly.

August 19, 2017 Move to the Wadsworth Auditorium and host two services without having enough room for everyone

January 27, 2018 Move to the Unity Auditorium

A S O N D J F M A M J J A S O N D J F M A M J J A S O N D J F M A M J J A S O N D
2016   2017   2018

Dreams start in the heart; guard it.

CHAPTER 1

AWAKENING DREAMS

CALEB

Austin and I first met on the side of the road at one o'clock in the morning back in 2012, four years before the night I sat writing dreams all over my glass coffee table. It's as crazy as it sounds.

We both grew up in the same small town in Georgia but had never met each other. A mutual mentor kept telling us individually that we needed to connect, but it wasn't until I recognized Austin's truck from behind that this meeting happened.

That night, I flashed my lights to get Austin to pull over—and he actually did. I introduced myself: "Hey, man, my name is Caleb Stanley. I heard you wanted to start something new here—so do I."

And that's how the idea for The Alternative was born—on the side of the road in the early hours of the morning. We were eighteen and nineteen years old, and we were just a couple of dreamers.

We weren't entirely sure how to chase our dream of doing something new in our community. Where would we even begin? But we knew this dream was something God wanted us to pursue, and He seemed to be bringing us together so we could pursue it as a team.

In the beginning, we had no plan, only passion. How do you plan for something that you have never done before? We wanted this to be organic. We wanted this to be authentic, and we were willing to sacrifice the five-year plan for a monthly analysis of our community's need. Investors didn't like this, but it felt right for us.

Planning for something you've never done before is like trying to draw a map of a road you've never traveled. It's uncertain and scary. But there's also something about stepping into the unknown that's exciting. It draws you in and introduces you to new people and new places on your journey toward your yet-unseen destination.

Although there was uncertainty, Austin and I did feel sure of one thing: there was a particular need in our community. We knew our friends and peers needed something to do on Saturday nights. Most had no real plans for the future, no vision for their lives. Ultimately, they had no hope. Some were stuck in destructive cycles—drug addiction, unhealthy relationships, you name it.

Surely there was something more we could be doing with our lives and our community—something positive, productive, and powerful. An alternative. Something that would invite new people in and establish unity.

What if . . . what if we could focus our vision on all those wasted Saturday nights? What if we could turn the emphasis away from short-lived parties and provide those around us a place to come together and find lasting hope? What kind of difference might that make in our community? In individuals' lives? In the world?

We had a dream in our hearts and the desire to chase after that dream, so we made a start, then and there. Many of you reading this may feel the same way. God has put a dream in your heart, but you have no idea how to follow it. You are not alone.

THE COST OF THE DREAM
GENESIS 37

Joseph was a dreamer. His dreams were visions sent directly from God. Not only did Joseph have a great relationship with God, he was his father, Jacob's, favorite son. With that much favor in his life, what could possibly go wrong?

Plenty. Joseph's brothers were deeply jealous of him. Sibling rivalry is never easy, and when parents pick an obvious favorite, it only compounds the problem. Joseph's brothers would grumble, "Here comes that dreamer," when he approached. Sounds like insecurity to me. They were not fans of his, to say the least, and they eventually sold their brother into slavery for a mere two weeks' wages.

But Joseph didn't let the price they put on him define his value. He knew he was worth more than what they said about him or how they treated him. He knew his worth. After all, he was a dreamer.

God had equipped Joseph to handle the adversity that his dreams would bring. Joseph's dreams were not mistakes, even though they cost him dearly. It's important to know that, just like Joseph, God's dream for us (our calling) is not a call to live in comfort, but a call to fulfill our purpose. God never fails to bring about His plan, and this is clear in the life of one of the Bible's most passionate dreamers.

DO SOMETHING ABOUT IT

What are you passionate about? A particular career? A relationship? School or sports? Friends or family? Growing in your faith? Art or music?

Maybe you used to be passionate about something, but the fire has faded. Maybe you're still passionate, but it feels like outside obstacles are stifling you, preventing you from pursuing what God has planned for you. Or maybe you haven't figured out what your passions are yet and you're looking around, wondering when it will be your turn to catch fire. That's okay.

The truth is, we all have a passion, even if it's momentarily lost, stifled, or hidden. But we can't just call it up at will. We must awaken it. How?

Find what hurts you. Find what compels you. Find what frustrates you. Find what moves you. In doing so, you'll stir up passions, and those passions will spark dreams. Just know that it takes courage to go to these places in your heart. These places might be covered by regret, or even past hurts. But you still need to take a deep look at your passion. It can become your greatest power if you let it. The places where you've been hurt the deepest are often the places where God will use you the most.

Dreams are God's gift to humanity—visions for what our futures could be like. God has *called* us to dream. Throughout God's Word, He tells us to have faith, to have courage, not to be afraid. He tells us to *go!* He says to rise. He calls us out into the unknown—to walk on water, through the sea, toward our giants, and past our greatest mistakes. He calls us to renew our minds and our hearts. He calls us to dream again.

What's your secret dream? We all have one. Sometimes it gets buried beneath fear of failure or the shame of past attempts. We lose our courage because we focus more on regret and hurt than on hope and potential. But your dream is your personal road map to *purpose* in your life. Isn't that what we all want—compelling purpose? For our lives to mean something, to truly matter?

But you must be honest with yourself. Your dream can't be your parents' hope for your life. It can't be something you pursue to gain recognition from others. To truly find purpose in your dreams, you must listen carefully to what God has put in your heart.

Dreams come in all shapes and sizes. Do you have a deep desire to help a hurting family member or friend? Do you want to start a nonprofit, be the first person in your family to go to college, or be a pioneer in your field? Those are dreams. Are your dreams wrapped around someone you love? Someone who's hurting? Is it a ministry? A business?

We're going to challenge you right now. We challenge you to look at your dreams as real possibilities, not as crazy notions that are outside your reach. Entertain the thought for a moment that maybe—just maybe—God has put these desires in your heart to serve as a road map to your destiny.

Throughout history, God has moved mightily in the lives of ordinary people. He meets us in moments of courage and vulnerability. For Peter, it was when he stepped out onto the water. For Moses, it was when he finally rose up to free his people. For Joseph, it was when he claimed the promise he'd always believed he had.

Dreaming doesn't mean you have a perfect plan. It means you are willing to go without one. You don't have to be well-known. You don't have to be recognized. You just have to be passionate. You just have to be you!

So, what's in your heart that you know you've hidden? What dormant passion needs to be reignited? What is it you want to wake up again—or maybe discover for the first time?

That thing that keeps you up at night—you know the one—are you going to dismiss it forever? No. You're not going to settle for less. You're not going to be content with yesterday. You're going to be courageous and vulnerable. You're going to give yourself permission to pursue the alternative. You're going to find what makes you feel alive in that intersection between your hope and God's plan. People are waiting on you.

Because *you* are a dreamer.

PERMISSION TO DREAM—CREATE A DREAM BOARD

When was the last time you let your dreams run wild? When was the last time you made those wild dreams take concrete shape in front of you? Let's do it now.

You can create a physical dream board with a corkboard and pushpins, or, let's be real, you can make it digital and keep it on your phone. Whatever you like. A private Pinterest board or even something as simple as notes with images pasted into them is great. Do what works for you.

Think about your passions, your hopes, things that keep you

up at night. Collect pictures that remind you of those dreams. Write your dreams down in a journal that you can keep near for times when you are filled with doubt and tempted to lose hope. Follow people on social media who are living these dreams. Begin to surround yourself with the people you want to be like. You duplicate what you see and who you surround yourself with.

There are other small steps you can take today. When I decided I wanted to be a leader, I asked my youth pastor to mentor me. Find someone to mentor you. Take a step back and examine your life, examine your friends. Do the people around you push you toward your dreams or pull you away from them? Maybe it's time to surround yourself with dreamers and believers, people who are hopeful for the future, leaders who are a couple steps ahead of you and can guide you on your journey.

It's important to keep the vision in front of you because passions will come and go, but your calling is here to stay. Remember that.

DREAMS CAN START SMALL

BY JORDAN KING

In July of 2011, I found myself on a bus headed to Panama City, Florida. The destination was a Christian resort, and I was about to experience the most important week of my life.

I was on vacation with my family when my aunt, uncle, and cousins invited me to a youth ministry's beach camp. If I wanted to go, I had a spot, but I needed to decide quickly because the camp began in two weeks. Naturally, I hated the idea of going to the beach for a whole week with a bunch of strangers, and on top of that, I didn't know where I stood as a Christian. But something deep inside of me told me to go. I remember speaking this to God. I said, "God, if You're real, if You have a plan for my life, if You really do love me, then show me at this camp. Show me who You are. This is Your one shot. Do not let me down."

I took a leap of faith. Against every fiber of my being, against everything that came naturally to me as an introverted sixteen-year-old, I decided to go on the trip.

So there I was, on a bus, on the way to the beach, with a bunch of people I didn't know. I was sitting with a camp counselor at the front of the bus, probably listening to music or sleeping, when my aunt walked down the aisle to get my attention. There was someone she wanted me to meet. I got up and followed her back a few rows to a guy standing there waiting to meet me. I shook his hand, said, "Hey, man, I'm Jordan." He replied, "Hey! I'm Caleb."

Little did I know that Caleb Stanley would soon become a great friend, a brother, the best man in my wedding, and someone I would dream with for the rest of my life.

I believe dreams all start in a similar place: God loves when we do things that make us a little uncomfortable, and He loves when we trust Him to see us through that experience. It's in these moments, when you lack vision and when you don't understand what God is up to, that the dream is planted and slowly, over time, begins to grow. In the beginning, you might not even know what the dream is, what it's called, or that the seed has even been planted, but in time, you look at whatever dream has been growing and it begins to make sense. For me, it started off very simply. I did something I didn't want to do and I trusted God through it. Now I can look back at that week of my life and know that was where my dreams began.

Between that week and now, God has taken me on an incredible adventure. After that camp, I started leading at my church and serving wherever I could. I graduated high school and started dating a girl who would become my wife. In July 2014, I headed to Sydney, Australia, to attend Hillsong College, where I spent a year learning from great leaders and friends who helped shape me into a godly man. In 2016, God began to speak to Caleb and Austin about reviving The Alternative (which they originally had started in 2012), and in the fall, we met once a week to worship and pray for The Alternative's relaunch event in January 2017. All those years, all the experiences, all the people I met, and all the things I learned have contributed to the dream God planted inside me. When I look back on all those things, I see the faithfulness of God. I see what He was up to. I see that the beach camp I attended was for a reason and that there was a reason I met a stranger named Caleb.

Dreams are a journey, and here's the cool thing about dreaming with God: it never stops. You never peak. God wants more out of you, and He wants more glory for Himself. Ephesians 3:20–21 says, "Now to him who is able to do immeasurably more than all we ask or imagine, according to his power that is at work within us, to him be glory in the church and in Christ Jesus throughout all generations, for ever and ever! Amen." God has done great things through the dream He planted in Caleb and Austin's hearts and through their willingness to chase after it. Lucky for me, I get to go along for the ride, and my personal dreams have started to intertwine with their dreams and with The Alternative's dream as a ministry. But here's the key: you must believe in yourself, believe in God, and believe in His word for dreams to begin and grow. No matter where The Alternative goes from here, every-thing we do and everything God gets glory for is happening because we all had a "beach camp" moment. A moment where, despite not fully understanding what God was doing, we decided to trust Him. You don't have to know all the details; you simply have to trust. The dream will begin to grow.

CHAPTER 2

DOES ANYONE SEE ME

CALEB

Nowadays, I am traveling much more, and when I am home it feels like I am either in a meeting or getting ready for an event. But it sure didn't start like this.

When we first met back in 2012, Austin and I both felt called to serve the church with our lives, but we didn't really understand what that would look like. To be honest, we still don't totally understand! We thought our work might look like what others were doing. At first, we thought maybe we could be the next Passion Conference or Hillsong Church.

We might have had a big dream, but we didn't realize yet the value of our specific callings. God didn't want a duplicate of something He'd already created. He wanted *us*.

But we didn't feel special. We were working at the church we'd grown up in, basically as janitors. Okay, they were nice and called us the Facilities Team because that sounded a little better. We would show up to prepare for our Wednesday night High School Gathering, Fusion, at one o'clock in the afternoon. First, we'd set up all five hundred chairs, clean the portion of the building where a Christian school met during the day, and then we would tidy up everything after the evening gathering was over.

We wiped toilets, took out the trash, and locked up room 208, where adult small groups would always run late. I remember staying up until two in the morning sometimes. We were both pursuing communications degrees at the time and had to attend class an hour away the next day. We would only get a couple hours of sleep.

Does anyone even see this? I wondered. *Surely all this work is worth a lot more than $64 a week . . .*

Negative thoughts hounded me during those early months. *No one sees this. No one cares. This is what I'm called to do?*

I didn't understand at all. God said I had a big calling on my life. But if He really created me with purpose, why was I spending my time cleaning toilets? It just didn't line up.

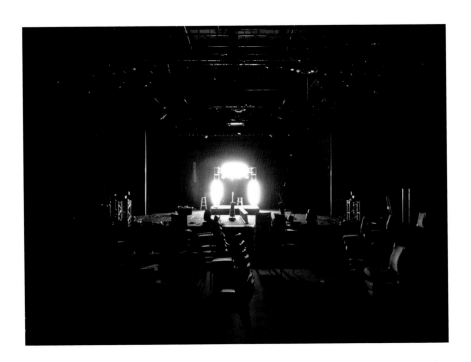

I felt forsaken. I felt like I wasn't valued by the leaders in my life. And it's easy to feel left behind and disempowered when the people around you haven't noticed you and your hard work. But those people—the hard-working ones in the background who are so often overlooked—those are the people God seems to favor.

One Friday, I had mowed the church lawn, like I always did, but because we had our first Alternative gathering the next day, I hadn't had time to blow the leaves from the parking lot. Saturday night, after our event, Austin and I flipped on our car headlights so we could see, and we spent two and a half hours blowing leaves in the dark, just to make sure we got it done before the church's service the next day.

Yes, that was our first poster!

That night in 2012 when we launched our Alternative gatherings was the start of something huge in our hearts. No longer was this journey just a dream. It was a reality—a really messy, very unprofessional reality, with ugly flyers and noisy fog machines. Seriously, it was rough.

But even in the midst of our inexperience, God was moving. We didn't know how to run sound or program lights, but the Holy Spirit was already at work. At that first gathering, we knew this was going to be bigger than ourselves. It had to be; otherwise, no one would want to come.

I was reminded in those early moments that you don't have to understand the entire plan or see the whole picture. You just have to step out and go for it. We didn't know all the details. It just felt right for us. A couple of kids accepted Jesus through those gatherings, so our hearts were full.

In the following years, we would see God grow the ministry to

Our first event's turnout.

reach over one hundred fifty different churches in twenty-seven states and outgrow every public building we could find in our city, leaving us with no option but to use the biggest building there, an older church with sixteen hundred seats.

But I couldn't have foreseen any of that in the early months of The Alternative. All I could see was the toilets we were scrubbing and the lawns we were mowing. Maybe you can relate.

If we're not doing what we feel called to do, does that mean we're missing something? Did we lose God somewhere a couple steps back? It's important to realize that doubt and discouragement are a part of the journey. Allow the tension of where you are help prepare you for all that's still ahead.

THE GIANT-SLAYING SHEPHERD
2 SAMUEL

King David rose to some pretty serious success in his life. (You noticed the "king" part, right?) He was also the guy who slayed giants. He rescued Israel in more ways than one, but he was also the kid who started in the field as a shepherd. No one followed him. No one talked about him. He was just a little shepherd boy.

He was the younger brother with less potential. Success in life was supposed to be for his older brothers, right? David's role was to tend the sheep, nothing more.

There was nothing special about being a shepherd. It wasn't a job to brag about. The sheep smelled. The days were exhausting. The nights were restless. The summer heat was intense. Oh, and you had to be away from your family for extended periods of time. Not ideal.

Other animals would prey on the sheep, and the shepherd was the only line of defense. Predators were dangerous. Being the only human with lots of sheep was lonely and isolating.

But David loved being a shepherd. He embraced his role with great commitment and dedication. David risked his life as he fought off lions to keep his sheep safe. David knew in his heart that just because others don't see you, it doesn't mean God has forgotten you.

It wasn't an accident that God put David in the role of a shepherd. David had a calling on his life—a calling to lead, protect, watch over, and fight. What if God put the lion in David's path to prepare him for Goliath, and placed David in the role of shepherd to prepare him to lead an entire nation?

What if the solitude David experienced in the fields helped him develop a deep intimacy with God? What if navigating the plains of Israel through the night prepared David to navigate the seasons of darkness in his own life? What if being the underdog in his family taught David that God measures success differently than peers and even family members do?

What if God had a plan for David the entire time?

DO SOMETHING ABOUT IT

Where you're headed matters. The goal matters. The dream is important. But so is the path to get there.

God often takes us on a roundabout journey, not just straight to a destination. Yes, we should hope for tomorrow, but that doesn't mean we should be so focused on what's ahead that we forget about what's happening today.

That process isn't always glamorous. Sometimes, it looks a whole lot like hard, unnoticed work—all those little things nobody sees. Everyone sees the big, game-winning home run, but do they see the hours of training and practice that went into that winning play? Everyone notices the perfect score on your final exam, but did they see the late nights of studying that made the A+ possible?

I'm not going to lie. The final destination looks great. The attention that comes with success sounds wonderful. The spotlight is appealing. Even those of us with stage fright would probably agree that the stage is an exciting place, and even if we are too afraid to stand on it, we admire those who do.

There's something about being *seen*. There's something about being *noticed* that entices us. Social media has given us the opportunity to be seen by people all over the world, and for a while, the likes and comments may fill our need to feel validated and accomplished. But in reality, our generation feels more isolated and lonely than any generation before us.

When I was younger, Facebook had just become the new thing. Every day after school, I would come home to check my notifications. But then, after fifteen minutes, social media was done for the day. I unplugged and went and did something else—homework, youth group, dinner with my family, hanging out with friends. These days, we don't always take that time to unplug because we have access everywhere we go on our phones. Technology has given us limitless possibility to connect and engage with the world, but often at the expense of engaging in deeper connections with those around us.

We get stuck in a cycle of comparison. Where is she? What is he doing tonight? Why wasn't I invited? Our profiles become more like portfolios, showcasing our best moments, our smiles and laughter, our best outfits, and our most popular friends, while ignoring the difficult or boring parts of our lives. We want to be seen, and we want to look good, often at the cost of embracing who we were really designed to be.

Being noticed seems to distract us from ourselves. It doesn't eliminate the pain or doubts we're dealing with, but it shifts our focus onto something else—the person we always wanted to be.

Maybe if we were a little more talented, a little more attractive, maybe we could be noticed too. But is that how God sees it? Is that how we are called to live? If it is, then we need to polish up our talents. We need to work harder to rack up our achievements if we ever want to step into this whole "dream" thing and fulfill our callings from God. We need to try harder and do more.

Except . . . that is not the gospel. God isn't looking for popular or good-looking. God isn't qualifying us based on what we have accomplished. He's looking for something else, something deeper.

We're not judged by how many trophies we've won or how much influence we've built. We're not judged by how quickly we get a job after college or what our paycheck looks like. Yeah, it's great to be successful, but true success isn't counted in dollars or likes or awards. It's counted in how we show love to the people around us. How we remain faithful to our dreams and our beliefs. How we stay patient in the face of setbacks and exercise self-control when we want to take a shortcut through life. It's counted in how we show joy, kindness, and passion in everything we do.

Some of us have dreams we will reach soon, and some of us have dreams we will be working toward for the rest of our lives. The timing isn't what's important. It's the way we go through the journey that matters most.

Do your best to be faithful in what God has called you to. Embrace the process.

Whether your life is glamorous or not, whether you look like the world's idea of success or not, just do your best to be faithful in what God has called you to. Embrace the process. Even if it's just mowing the church lawn for $64, believe that what you are doing really does matter, even if no one sees it.

If you have a goal you want to accomplish, it's not going to happen overnight. It may not happen where, when, or even how you thought it would. Locations change, titles change, brands change, strategies change, but the reason you started following your dream doesn't have to. Our callings *never* change. God sees the big picture—He sees the process from start to finish, and He sees the end goal. He has a plan to help us chase the dreams He's put in our hearts.

Knowing that God sees us and has a plan is crucial to staying the course. If you have a big goal in mind, you're going to face hardship—

probably a lot of it. But you can take those hardships as an opportunity to learn. Each setback today is a way to prepare for tomorrow, no matter how hard it may seem, no matter how small or unimportant the task may appear, no matter how unappreciated you feel.

God wants us to dream. He wants us to think about the future. Even as we journey faithfully through the "right now," and even as we face hardships, God is calling us forward.

And maybe what He's given you today is something small— like scrubbing toilets. One of the biggest red flags for me is to hear people ask if they can have a moment in the spotlight when those same people don't show up to serve. Or they don't even show up to any meetings. Anyone who *only* seeks the stage concerns me. Watch out for these people.

The people who stay committed to the little things, those who put others before themselves—those are the kind of people God is looking for, the kind of people He can work through in a big way. Don't try to force your way out of the field and into the palace. Keep shepherding, keep trusting. God will come get you when it's time.

EMBRACING THE PROCESS—JOURNALING

We are all waiting for something. We all want that promotion, that acceptance letter, that first big title. But rather than focusing all our energy on where we want to be, let's embrace where we are. Grow in gratitude by thanking God for the opportunities you do have.

Where has God placed you right now? What's your starting point? Grab your favorite journal, a notebook, a piece of paper, or even a sticky note. Write down a list of five things in your life right now that you can embrace. Maybe you're not where you ultimately want to end up, but jot down what's good about *right now*. Think of ways you can grow while you're in this stage of your life. You will never get today back, so don't miss an opportunity!

CAN ANYONE SEE ME?

BY NIGEL WALLACE

In a world full of people who want to make an impact, our God
is always looking for those who want to be used by Him. At
a glance, this can be a lovable idea for anyone. I mean, who
wouldn't want to be used by God, as a light to be shined in this
world full of darkness? Unfortunately, dreams can die, and hearts
can be broken after acknowledging the hefty set of terms and
conditions that come with laying down your own plans in attempt
to pick up God's.

For several reasons, our eager eyes and hungry hearts
love seeing things accomplished by the fulfillment of our own
strength.

Many people take words like *insignificant* and *unnoticed* and
allow them to be the two overarching narratives that label their
lives. Others fight for acceptance and pray for influence, impact,
and a "platform." While these prayers may be eager and earnest,
there is a tendency to allow our hearts to become unsteady,
especially when we are "patiently" awaiting the provision we
have prayed for.

We have all fought hard against the friction of life and have
done everything we could to put our dent in the sphere of the
world. We push the envelope, go through the motions, and share
all that we can on social media, trying to achieve some sort of
spiritual significance. We all have the desire to share our dreams
with the world and grace others with the gifts God gave us.

The problem is, the world isn't always down to buy what we
are selling. And we let that defeat us by living under the concern
of how other people view us, letting their acceptance and opinion be the driver that keeps our vehicle moving forward. But God

has never been concerned with how we look, or how hard we've worked to achieve things.

God wants to bless our tomorrow, but we cannot be quiet in honoring Him today. God's main concern is not exposing (or utilizing) the calling He has placed over our lives. None of our ideas of significance can be unlocked or "achieved" until He has complete access to the inner workings and overall posture of our hearts.

In 1 Samuel 13:13–14, God declares that He will grant the kingdom of Israel to a man after His own heart. This holds truth that there is a special blessing that awaits the soul of a man (or woman) who is pursuing God's own heart.

How did David, a servant and shepherd boy who looked after a flock of sheep in a field—who was passed over seven times before becoming Israel's anointed king—actually become the king of Israel?

David was refined during his season in the field. He was a good steward of what he had been gifted. He was faithful over few. He abandoned the ideas of selfishness and fulfillment of his flesh, and he was humbled by the things he suffered through. David witnessed God's favor over his life as he delighted in the Lord, his God.

But we can't jump straight into David being king without acknowledging the significance of his shepherding.

A shepherd's primary responsibility is the welfare of his or her flock. God has a herd for all of His children to bear—and calls us to take exceptional care of that herd, whether doing so feels hindering, uplifting, or unconventional. We can't expect to carry a heavier load publicly if we poorly handle the responsibility He has given us privately.

We ARE seen in our seasons of invisibility—by God Himself. That is the beauty that hard seasons of life brings. They show us that opinions and perspectives of other people are insignificant when placed in comparison to the perspective of God. Living in the world, but not being of it, is not easy, but sometimes your spiritual development is as simple as shepherding the sheep you have been given.

CHAPTER 3

BUILT TO BUILD

AUSTIN

While I was growing up, my dad and I worked on a lot of projects together. Whether it was changing the brakes in the car or working on the tractor or building tree stands, I was always by his side, building and fixing.

I figured out early on that I love to build things. I love the concept of creating something from scratch. Whenever we were working on a project and would get to a spot where we didn't have the right tool, we would improvise somehow. We'd make it work and finish the job. Building and creating have been in my blood my whole life.

As I moved into my late teenage years, I started to think about ways I could generate an income for myself. Instead of getting a "normal" job at a local restaurant or retail store, I got creative and opened a woodworking business.

I knew woodworking wouldn't be my main income, but I figured it could potentially become a great side business for me. And why not earn money doing work I truly enjoyed?

I was in the garage one day when I came across an old hand router. Hand routers are used for hollowing out small sections of wood, especially when making furniture. This router had been sitting on the shelf for years without me ever understanding what it was meant for. But I picked it up and started playing with it.

I carved into some pallet wood I had acquired for firewood. Then I found some stencils that were lying around and started engraving Bible verses and sayings into the wood. When I decided to throw my new creations on Facebook, the post blew up. Messages poured in. People wanted custom signs made for their homes. The business grew.

Over the next few years, my dad and I invested in a machine that makes the carving process a little easier. After we had been making custom signs for a few years, we decided to branch out and build custom dining room tables. We both have a passion for building things, and we figured we would be able to turn a little bit more profit for my family if we expanded into larger wood-working projects. Making signs is fun, but why not go for it and be open to a whole new market?

If you've worked with wood before, you know you get one chance. Only one. A single mistake can ruin a whole project, and once you make that mistake, you very likely will have to start over again.

Not gonna lie; I've been frustrated many times because a mistake—my *single* mistake—destroyed weeks of work. Usually the error happened because I wasn't paying attention. I wasn't alert about what was going on, so I slipped up.

After we began to broaden our customer base, I felt a lot of pressure to make sure I was creating beautiful products so our customers would feel like they got their money's worth, and then some. I never wanted anyone to regret hiring me.

This particular table was extra special. It was big—nine feet long by three feet wide, with six different legs. My customer wanted the base of this beast to be made of steel, with two-inch steel tubing as legs.

So we bought all the materials we needed. We cut the right length for the legs, making sure we weren't even an eighth of an inch off. If we were off a tiny bit on one piece, the finished project would be off by a lot. After we got the legs and base pieces cut, we got to welding.

This was the fun part. Have you ever played connect the dots? Building furniture is a little like that. We could finally see our work come together. We welded one leg to the base, then another and another and another, and voila! We ended up with a base and six legs.

After we put the base and legs together, all we had left to do was build the top. Now, don't think this was the easy part. This was actually the most difficult element to make happen. After buying the right wood—not only the correct type but the best pieces we could find—we had to cut them down to size, hoping we didn't make a dumb mistake and ruin the wood. Then we had to get all the pieces in the correct order they needed to be on the table.

Everything was flowing perfectly for this table. The base and top went together like peas and carrots. I got it glued and sanded, then off to staining we went. After applying a couple coats of the customer's desired stain, we began applying polyurethane to the table. Polyurethane is a finish for wood products that seals and protects the wood, giving it a nice, smooth finish.

I applied the first coat to the tabletop, and it looked just right. It smoothed out perfectly. No bugs were in it, which was amazing. You see, once you put a coat of finish down, there's no going back. If you put a coat of finish down and a bug or some dust or other pieces of debris from inside the shop get on it, you can't just pluck it out and move on. You have to let it dry and then sand it down enough to get the dust or bug out.

So, I was thrilled with the smooth, perfect finish I had going at this point. I left it to sit overnight with great expectations. It was going to need one more coat, but it was going to look incredible. The table was almost complete.

The next day, I woke up and made my way to the garage. And there they were. A flock of evil gnats were stuck all over the polyurethane.

I was so mad. The table had been perfect—and so close to being done!

My mind started spinning with damage control ideas.

I'll use high-grit sand paper to get them off.

That made it worse. The bug-infested tabletop now had smear marks all over it. My mind went into overdrive.

This table is due tomorrow. I'm doomed. The customer is going to say she doesn't want it anymore. She's going to hate it.

What am I going to do?

JERUSALEM'S BUILDER
BOOK OF NEHEMIAH

Nehemiah was cupbearer to King Artaxerxes of Persia. We might not realize this, but the cupbearer was a really important position. He went everywhere the king went, and he was the one who tasted the king's food and drink to make sure no one had poisoned it. The king trusted the cupbearer with his life.

Nehemiah was living pretty well, but then he learned about the wall of Jerusalem. Some of Nehemiah's fellow Israelites had returned to their homeland, but the rebuilding of their capital city wasn't going well. Nehemiah saw the massive need of his people, and he wanted to help. God gave him a dream to go to Jerusalem to rebuild the wall that surrounded the city.

As Nehemiah prepared to go to the city, he had to be careful of every move he made. If he selected the wrong people for his team, they might end up hindering the project, rather than helping it. If he wasn't careful about each step of the process, he might make a catastrophic error and have to start over. Just like in woodworking, one mistake could spell disaster for Nehemiah's project.

Nehemiah left his comfortable life of service to the Persian king to pursue the vision God had put in his heart. What if it didn't go perfectly? (It didn't.) What if Nehemiah faced obstacles? (He did.) But the vision was too important for him to give up on. His people were counting on him.

Nehemiah was building the wall of the most important city in Judah. What are you building today?

DO SOMETHING ABOUT IT

Have you ever had a self-inflicted issue? For instance, you think you're being creative, solving problems, but you're actually just messing things up more? That was me with this table.

In those times where you're building something and you make a mistake, do you think to yourself, "Is it even worth it to start over? Is it even worth it to fix it?" Maybe you weren't building a physical object, like I was, but we've all been there. You're working hard toward something, then you hit a major detour and you're not sure it even makes sense to keep going toward your goal.

I had those thoughts about that table. Then I took a step back for a moment and stared at my polyurethane-coated bugs. *Maybe I should call somebody? Ah-ha! I know! YouTube!* Surely YouTube would save me. Someone would have a hack that would fix it all.

Starting over ... and the final result.

But every video I found suggested removing all the finish and stain and starting over.

Starting over—*from scratch.*

No way! Not happening! I couldn't afford to lose all that time. I prayed over the table and left it overnight, hoping for a miracle. When I returned the next morning, with next-level faith, the bugs and scratches were still there. Defeated, I removed every scrap of stain and finish.

After it was complete, I was tired, and I was upset by my failure. But guess what? The new tabletop ended up being more beautiful than the first. The process was frustrating and uncomfortable, but the finished product was so rewarding. I was a few days late on my order, but I'd made a beautiful product and the customer was happy (thank goodness!). I met my goal—with a lot of bumps along the way.

What's your end-goal dream? At this point, you've probably thought about it a bit. Maybe you've created a dream board, like Caleb suggested in chapter 1, and it helped you visualize your goal.

My short-term goal was building a beautiful table for my customer, but I've had lots of bigger dream-goals in my life too. When I think back on the process of building that table, it's impossible not to compare it to what it's been like to pursue my bigger dream-goals in life, which have included both the thrills of success and the dismay of waking up to find my plans thwarted.

Are you taking concrete steps toward some of your dream-goals yet? Are you sketching out your table design or selecting the perfect piece of wood to get started? Maybe you're even in the beginning stages of building, of fitting together those beautiful pieces of wood. Maybe you've even run into some surprise gnats already. Even if you're not taking these concrete steps yet, you're still building something. We all are. Perhaps you're working on building your character. That character-building might be a key part of your journey so you can handle the dream when it's time to start working on that. The personal growth is what will see you through the worst gnat infestations.

Are you taking concrete steps toward some of your dream-goals?

But no matter where you are or what you're doing, God is building something *in* you and *through* you to create a huge impact.

BORN TO BUILD—MAKE SOMETHING

We're born to create things. Some people like to make things in the kitchen. Some people like to make things in their gardens. Some people like to create stories or write music or draw pictures.

For this activity, let's try *building* something. That might mean shopping at the hardware store or the craft store—either is fine. The goal is to find a project you can do that involves putting together something physical, piece by piece. (If you're really stuck, they sell kits for kids—I won't tell anyone.)

As you work, notice how you must pay attention to each step of the process, taking care so you don't make a big mistake and wreck your project. And if you do wreck your project somehow? Don't give up! Go back to the beginning if you have to, but keep trying.

Notice how every step is important to reach your end goal. And notice how sometimes, in the middle of the process, you can't even tell what that final project is going to look like. Sometimes you have to keep going and see it through to the end before you get the big picture. As you work through your project, think about the parallels between your project and your dream.

THE SLEDGEHAMMER LESSON

BY BRIAN PRESTON

In the summer of 1990, I was helping my grandfather, Lamon Luther Wilson, build a barbed-wire fence on his farm. It was my first experience building anything from the ground up, and I was excited, to say the least.

It was a *hot* July Saturday. My grandpa asked me to help him gather the necessary tools. One tool in particular was a large and heavy sledgehammer. I mean, I didn't know it was called a sledgehammer at the time; I just knew this beast of a tool would create a massive amount of energy and force, and the object to be "sledged" didn't stand a chance of survival. I wondered what my grandpa was going to be using this kind of hefty hammer for. I worked up all the strength a child could possibly possess, and I helped my grandpa load the tools into the back of his pickup truck.

We started with the layout, and then we stretched a string from one lead post to another. "If you're going to do something, take the time to plan and do it right the first time," my grandpa said. Over the next twenty years, this was a lesson he loved to teach me.

The next task was installing the poles. He didn't use the sledgehammer to do this. He used a standard hammer to get the pole started in the ground. Then it was my time to shine. "Hold this pole, son," he said. The pole was green with a white tip. I put my death grip on it, and then he reached for that sledgehammer. "Hold this pole, son," he said again, "as I knock it in the ground." He started hammering the pole into the ground, and the hammer head would slip off the pole every couple times. My grandpa was a big man. He looked like a giant with that sledgehammer.

One time, the hammer slipped off the pole and got really close to my head. "Pa, you're going to hit me in the head!" I screamed.

"Son, don't be afraid. I would never hit you in the head. Hold it tight, now!"

"Can we go back to the smaller hammer? It seems safer."

"We will never get this fence done by using the smaller hammer, son."

And then he said something I'll never forget: "Son, if things are hard in this life, you're probably using the wrong tools."

For the record, my grandpa did whack me on the head that day. I think I laid on the ground for a good fifteen minutes, and I'm pretty sure I blacked out. But he taught me the importance of using the right tool that day—despite fear, despite risk, and despite the possibility of head injury.

I love how Austin reminds us in this chapter that we are all building something. Because we are created in the image of the Creator, we are programmed to think like builders. It's part of our genetic makeup to build. Have you ever noticed that many of the oldest artifacts we've found from ancient civilizations are tools? We are created to build, to craft, to make . . . but the tools we use will define us. Throughout history, God has given human beings visions and innovation to create solutions and help make jobs easier. Pick the right project to build, and most importantly, pick the right tools.

You will be remembered by what you build in this life. One day we will all die, but things we build while on earth have the potential to impact eternity and to be remembered forever.

CHAPTER 4

DON'T COME DOWN

AUSTIN

Back in 2012, Caleb and I saw a need in our city, Newnan, Georgia. People desperately desired to see God in a new way. And once we kicked off a monthly event on the last Saturday of every month—the beginning of The Alternative—we started to see people's lives change. It wasn't us. It wasn't something *we* did. God was at work within our community.

Churches began to come together—churches that had been in the same town for fifteen years and had never worked together. It was a special time for the city.

After we had been running The Alternative for about two years, providing a place for people to freely worship God for what He was doing in their lives, we thought we had the vision for The Alternative down pat. We knew God had us here for a reason. We were seeing our ministry grow like crazy. We were moving to new, larger venues all the time. Keeping up with the demand for space was a challenge, and it was hard to find places that could house what was happening.

Then, in 2014, things began to go wrong: attendance started

to drop. We didn't know why people weren't coming back every month. Discouragement set in, and we began to feel defeated. We weren't seeing people hungry for God anymore. It made me question whether we were doing something wrong. Had we misunderstood the dream? Was our goal off the mark? Was something wrong with our execution?

Plain and simple, we didn't see the need in our community anymore. At least, we thought we didn't.

This is it, I thought. *It's not going to last. We've failed.*

The negative thoughts were difficult to swallow and caused us to shift our focus to where we thought it should be. In January 2015, Caleb took a job with a church. I took a youth pastor position a few months later at the same church. This required a move to a different, unfamiliar city.

That was tough. My heart was still in Newnan. My dream was still for God to move through The Alternative in Newnan. But I

Losing momentum, and we knew it.

also understood that Newnan might not be where God wanted me forever.

So, the move was tough but good. This new job challenged me in a way I'd never been challenged before. It was a time of massive personal growth for me, leaving behind a dream that had been in my heart—*our* hearts—for years. The Alternative felt like it was over and done with. But . . . I was still hopeful. Something told me we were only done for a little while.

I had no idea what the future might hold, but I knew The Alternative would be part of it. One day, Caleb and I were sitting in the church office, and we received a phone call from a political party in Switzerland. They wanted to buy our domain, thealternative.org, and offered us a lot of money. Caleb and I looked at each other and said no at the same time. We both knew. We knew The Alternative wasn't over.

Our best days were still ahead. And what felt like a setback—a momentary confusion—was actually just a setup for something bigger.

WARRIOR ON THE WALL
BOOK OF NEHEMIAH

When we left our story of Nehemiah in chapter 3, he was pursuing the dream God had given him of rebuilding Jerusalem's wall. No sooner did Nehemiah begin to pursue this calling than he started to experience setbacks.

First, Persia was 1,418 miles from Jerusalem. After Nehemiah finally made it to Jerusalem, he and his team were ready to get building.

But his next setback came in the form of resistance from others. I think we can all relate to that. A man named

Sanballat was very angry with Nehemiah for trying to rebuild Jerusalem's wall. Sanballat was a Samaritan, and Nehemiah was a Jew—there was a major culture clash happening.

Nehemiah and his team then had a choice: they could be distracted by the sarcastic remarks and threats of Sanballat, or they could stay focused. They were feeling the weight of pursuing their dream. The people began working on the wall with a tool in one hand and a weapon in the other. But they didn't let it slow them down.

Soon, it started to get real. Sanballat was plotting to kill Nehemiah and his team. This would be enough to derail most of us, but Nehemiah stayed focused on the work before him. He didn't come down from the wall.

Next, his team started to get worn out. They started to complain. Nehemiah faced the setback of negativity. But Nehemiah dealt with it like a leader. He showed those working with him how to press on and not lose sight of the dream.

The last and biggest setback Nehemiah faced was fear. Fear can paralyze us and prevent us from answering God's calling. For Nehemiah's team, it caused them to lose their motivation to finish their work. Can we blame them? Imagine you're laying bricks, and suddenly people are threatening to attack you—to kill you. All you have to fight back with is the tool you use to file bricks. That's a scary situation!

Instead of giving in to fear, Nehemiah told his team to grab their swords. He told them to continue God's work while defending themselves from outside attack. That's serious commitment and drive. That's a serious coming together of community, united in purpose and vision.

Like Nehemiah, we can fight through all the distractions,

combat all the setbacks, and keep our focus on our goals. Nehemiah didn't come down off that wall, and we don't have to either!

DO SOMETHING ABOUT IT

Have you ever experienced a setback? Most of us have experienced lots of small setbacks, but perhaps you've had a big one. Maybe everything was looking great. You had your perfect college picked out. You knew what and where you wanted to be in your life. And then it fell through.

Maybe you were dating someone, and you just knew that this was the one! Then everything changed, faster than you could comprehend. It hurt. It was confusing. Maybe you were on the fast track as an athlete. You were progressing, and people and schools were noticing you. Then the worst happened—an injury that changed the course of your athletic career forever.

We all face setbacks, large and small. Although they can be frustrating, disheartening, or even traumatic, setbacks today can prepare us for our tomorrow. We think we're moving backward, but really, it's like God has us in a slingshot. He's pulling us back for a moment to release us into tomorrow in a big way.

While setbacks can be God getting ready to slingshot us into our futures, they can become permanent if we allow ourselves to become distracted from our goals. Remember your dream? Remember your original vision? It's important to be open to allowing that vision to grow or change, as needed, but it's equally important that we don't allow ourselves to get totally sidetracked and stall out.

We can let the smallest things derail us. A stupid subtweet ruins our day, or we make a bad decision, like accepting an invite

While setbacks can be God getting ready to slingshot us into our futures, they can become permanent if we allow ourselves to become distracted from our goals. to a party with the wrong crowd. Sometimes getting sidetracked comes from the world around us, and sometimes it comes from our own decisions. Sometimes we listen to that little (or big) voice inside that whispers, *You can't do it.*

Don't listen to that voice. Don't let your setbacks stop you. Stay hopeful. Get back up, and do the work God has for you.

Stay alert! Don't let yourself lose focus. Those big dreams God has put in our hearts need our best work, our time, and our attention if we're going to see them realized.

Don't be tempted to give up. You might feel ready to throw in the towel right now. But understand that nothing can stop what God has started if we're willing to be brave about pursuing our dreams. Your setback today is your setup for the future.

SLINGSHOTTING FORWARD—MAKE A LIST

Are you feeling stuck right now? Maybe your big dream is on track, but you feel stuck in some other area of your life. That's okay. It's normal to get into ruts we'd like to escape, create bad patterns we'd like to break, or be sidetracked by distractions we want to ignore. The trick is not staying stuck in that place forever!

So, let's make a list. Grab your journal or a piece of paper and write down that one area in your life where you feel like you're experiencing the greatest setback. Now, as quickly as you can, brainstorm ten ways to get unstuck. Don't edit yourself. Just write down your first ten thoughts. Give yourself a minute to think about it, then write out five or ten more ideas.

Anything brilliant come to you? Sometimes writing a list of ideas as quickly as we can helps us get all the clichéd, unhelpful options out of our systems so we can break through to the really creative thinking. Your first five or seven ideas might not get you unstuck, but what about the others? See if there's something inspirational on your list, and go for it. Get out of that rut, break that pattern, reclaim your focus.

GOD'S TRAINING GROUND

MASEY MCLAIN

I started acting when I was fifteen years old. And once I was in high school, I knew the Lord was calling me into the entertainment business as a career. I went to a coffee shop with my mom one day and told her that deep down, I felt God was going to use me in entertainment in some way—I just didn't know how.

While most people see the perks of being an actor or performer, they usually don't realize there's a lot of rejection that comes along with the job. In college, I felt a constant tension between knowing what God had been calling me to do for many years and experiencing constant rejection in the pursuit of that goal. And I mean constant. I honestly didn't understand it at all, and I often let God know it. Why would he call me to do something and then never let me succeed? Little did I know, when God calls you to something, many times it does not come to fruition right away. I thought God was going to fling open the doors to my dreams—instead he catapulted me into a spiritual boot camp, a training ground that was brutal but crucial to my calling.

My freshman year of college, I was about to give up the whole acting dream I'd once felt God had placed in my heart. Why not try a more stable career, like being a teacher or a nurse? Why not try a nine to five? The problem was, none of those things made my heart come alive. My heart wasn't wired to do anything else, and deep down I knew it. But I was tired of the fight and I was tired of the rejection, and couldn't see how God was ever going to make a way for me to be a professional actress.

Shortly after I was getting ready to turn in the acting towel, I received an audition for a widely popular TV show. I told the Lord that this was going to be my last audition and that if I got it, I would know that He was in fact still calling me to this whole acting thing—despite my feelings and discouraged heart. I ended up booking the part. I packed up the car, headed to Nashville with my mom, and filmed my first episode with the whole cast. The part was my dream role—an upcoming singer who was pure of heart and was the "good girl" of the show the main character would later be threatened by. She was the rising star. I had always wanted to be on a show where I could sing and act, and it seemed like my dreams were coming true.

Filming was a surreal experience. I sat next to Hayden Panettiere in a makeup chair while the cast congratulated me and said, "Welcome to the family, you're a regular now!" After filming the first episode, I was given the impression I was going to be a big part of the storyline, so I went home and waited for them to tell me when it was time to come back for season two. When I finally got the call, it wasn't what I expected: "Hey, Masey, we just wanted to tell you that we loved you and it's nothing personal, but we're cutting your character and cutting your scene out of the episode. We decided to go a different direction with the story."

Talk about confusion and setback. I cried and I questioned and I was mad at God. Why would You call me to something and make it so unbelievably hard and heartbreaking? I remember standing in front of my mirror crying and asking Him why—and to my surprise, He answered me. It's difficult to explain how you hear God speak to you, but without a doubt I heard His voice: "How quickly would your heart change if I gave you everything you wanted right now? You say you're doing this for My glory, but is it just a mask for your own kingdom?" I felt like I had been punched in the gut, and knew He was right. I wasn't ready for what He was calling me to. My heart needed renovation. Work had to be done if I was going to truly step into what He had planned for me. That day I entered my training ground. The vision and the calling stayed—I still knew He had truly called me to the entertainment business, I just had to wait for His timing. And as my training progressed, I realized I'd desperately needed the setbacks, because they revealed the state of my heart and were tools to shape me. If the calling was as big as I had hoped, I had to be ready.

Don't lose the dream and don't lose sight of the calling. Don't let your setbacks distract you from what God's called you to—let them mold you and shape you. They're necessary, and they're part of your training. Stay focused and keep going.

CHAPTER 5

DON'T LOOK BACK

CALEB

Here's an important truth to understand: If you're a dreamer, you are going to be hurt. You are going to be let down. It's inevitable because you're a risk-taker. But you can't camp out in that place of hurt and disappointment. You must keep moving. As a visionary—someone who dreams and plans for tomorrow—if you get trapped in the *what ifs* of yesterday, you will never be able to walk in the *could bes* of your vision.

The past is tricky. It can be full of good memories, but it also can hold discouraging failures and painful lessons. Sometimes focusing on the past is what holds us back. Other times, people hold us back, even when they don't mean to. These people are usually only acting out of their own insecurity and pain, not out of malice. But the end result is the same—they're unwittingly holding us back from our goals.

I've learned this the hard way. I naturally trust people. I tend to believe people, especially people I care about. It's easy for me to hold on to what people have said about me—the promises they've made, the futures they've planned, or even the opinions people have so bluntly expressed. Those words stay with me.

Can you relate? Maybe those words were spoken to you by a friend, or a boyfriend or girlfriend. Maybe it was a parent. But just because they are close to you, that doesn't mean what they say has to be true for you.

During 2015, Austin and I left our home church and The Alternative to help a friend of mine, Josh Rhye, at ThreeLife Church. We both served on staff there, and it was a great time of refocusing and reprioritizing, remembering who we were and what God had called us to. But after that break, we decided to move back to Newnan and relaunch The Alternative. An older gentleman in my life heard about our plans. This individual was someone I listened to, someone I trusted. He told me that if we attempted to relaunch, our ministry would not last. He told me our plan might get a lot of initial hype, but it would eventually fall apart because we were not ready to sustain it.

At first, I was able to dismiss what he told me. But his words never really left me—they just got hidden behind the noise of all the growth. After several months passed, I was facing multiple emotional, organizational, and even family challenges, and his words would sneak back up. "It's going to fall apart. It's just hype. You never should have left."

Austin, Caleb, and Josh Rhye while at ThreeLife

What if he was right? I would ask myself. *What if I'm going to fail?*

When you're in your early twenties, you usually don't know how to lead well. Even if you do, the people you are leading are probably young and passionate (and reckless), so you get a lot of followers who really want to be part of what you're doing but may not be as committed to the long-term goal. After a short amount of time, they find problems—they don't feel valued, or they simply find the next "big thing" to move on to and be part of instead. It can be extremely difficult when the people you are leading transition or leave, because they often don't just leave the ministry—they leave *you*. When the ministry is your dream and you've given your life to it, it's personal.

Within the first year of relaunch, I lost several people close to me—some to death, some to moves, and some to life decisions. Amidst the growth of the ministry, I was doing everything I could just to keep up. Those words, "You won't be able to sustain the ministry," tormented me in my weakest moments.

We all are reminded at times about the words people have said to us and about us, especially when we're struggling to keep up. But you shouldn't let those thoughts stay, not even as a whisper in your mind. Fight them. Don't let a whisper fool you—despite its gentle delivery method, a whisper is extremely powerful. Those whispers plant seeds of doubt, and while seeds start out tiny, they can grow into something much bigger. Don't underestimate the power of a whisper.

Memories and whispers are a lot alike, aren't they? They are both powerful voices delivered in a very intimate way. They will creep in, often in our weakest moments, with a language that speaks to our inadequacy and weakness. They come at the same time every night, and they're the loudest whispers you've ever heard. So, what do you do? Is God's plan for your life just to endure these whispers?

No. We must turn away from the whispers that follow us.

Whatever it is that is holding you down, it's time to leave it in the past. Maybe you need to delete a phone number, unfollow some people on Instagram, change jobs. Maybe you need some accountability to help you leave behind that destructive behavior, or that destructive person who keeps creeping in on your life and your goals. Maybe you need to cancel some subscriptions or change the group of friends you confide in.

You can't keep dancing around the things that are trying to kill you. If you get trapped here, you may miss out on the vision God has put in your heart. Every great historymaker has had defining moments in their story where they have chosen to leave something behind in order to pick up something new. It might be leaving words behind. It might be leaving an identity behind. It might be leaving a person behind; it probably will at some point. Only you know.

We pushed through with our ministry, even in those moments of doubt. But it's easy to give up. I heard Steven Furtick (founder and pastor of Elevation Church in Charlotte, North Carolina) say once that he used to be impressed when people had the faith to start something, but ten years later, he was only impressed by the people who stayed committed. I get that. Starting is easy, especially for dreamers. But staying faithful to God's call on your life when people leave you, when their opinions talk louder than your confidence—that's hard. Real hard. Don't look back. Stay focused. Keep stepping.

> Whatever it is that is holding you down, it's time to leave it in the past.

THE PILE OF SALT NOBODY TALKS ABOUT
GENESIS 19

There are plenty of people who have looked back and gotten stuck in the past, so you've never heard their stories. But there is one individual who looked back and became famous for it. Her whole story is about looking back. Her name isn't given, and perhaps that's because she missed her purpose. What we do know is that she was married to a man named Lot.

Lot and his wife lived in the wealthy city of Sodom. Sodom was a broken place—broken people, broken sexuality, full of idols and crime. It was wealthy, but it was rough. God sent angels to save Lot and his family from Sodom before the city was destroyed for good. The only catch? As they fled, they couldn't look back.

Lot and his family listened. They left. They had almost no time to pack their memories. They charged into the valley and headed toward a small town called Zoar. But as they approached this new place, Lot's wife looked back toward Sodom and became a pillar of salt.

Wait, what? Yeah, that's right. She turned into salt.

Why did she look back when she had been instructed not to? Perhaps she didn't have the strength to leave behind all her memories. After all, she was practically forced to leave. But whatever the reason, her heart stayed in the past.

When we stay in the past, our purpose is on the line. Our future—our dream—is at risk. We must look forward, or else we might very well end up with a pillar of salt instead of our big vision.

DO SOMETHING ABOUT IT

We all have things in our past that are trying to keep us from our future. Thoughts that tell us we have no hope—that because of our mistakes and inadequacies, our potential is gone. As dreamers, we can't focus on these thoughts. Your emotional well-being can't depend on events from your past—whether those events were failures or harsh words spoken by others. You don't have time to entertain them. You don't have time to listen to everyone's opinions about how you will win or lose. They weren't given your life, so stop letting them live it. That's easier said than done, of course.

Think about it for a second. What from your past do you keep looking back to? What from your past do you keep listening to? Maybe you're trying to escape those words, but no matter how hard you try, the thoughts still come back.

These negative thoughts can paralyze us, but they aren't the truth. Think about some of history's biggest "failures." Imagine if they had allowed themselves to be trapped in their pasts. They could have. But they didn't. They were some of the world's most ambitious dreamers, and they didn't allow themselves to remain in the past.

The Wright Brothers. They weren't just the first to fly a powered aircraft . . . they were among the first to crash one. Multiple times. They broke the bank replacing parts and funding their adventures. They started in a bicycle shop, not some glamorous factory. Months went by, and they moved cities to find the right wind. The Wright

Orville and Wilber Wright

Brothers were mocked. I mean . . . airplanes? Hah. Not possible. But years of disbelief were proven wrong with just twelve seconds of flight time in 1903. You'd be amazed at how quickly the tables can turn for the dreamers.

Michael Jordan

Michael Jordan. If you don't know who Michael is, he's arguably the best basketball player of all time. I feel like every fourth shoe I see someone wearing is a type of Jordan. Although he went on to be one of the most successful athletes of all time, he didn't make his high school varsity basketball team. But he stayed focused on his future, which allowed him to set countless NBA records that some of the world's greatest athletes today still strive to match.

Henry Ford. Ford didn't just create one of the most popular motor companies to date—he also created multiple failed business, all of them leaving him broke, before he founded the Ford Motor Company. His perseverance went on to change the world.

Henry Ford

Albert Einstein. We know him as a genius.

Albert Einstein

But Einstein didn't speak until he was four years old. He didn't read until he was seven. His teachers thought he had a learning disability. He was expelled from his school as a teenager. That's not exactly what we'd imagine the path of a Nobel Prize winner to look like. But he didn't let those obstacles define him.

Thomas Edison. Edison was told he was too stupid to learn anything. I'd like to think that every invention he imagined was his way of proving the doubt in his heart wrong. Did you know he was fired from his first two jobs because he

Thomas Edison

wasn't "productive enough"? Aren't you glad Thomas Edison didn't look back—especially if you're reading this under a light?

Stan Smith. You know those Adidas tennis shoes everyone has been wearing for what feels like forever, Stan Smiths? Yep, it's the same guy—a famous tennis player. Smith was rejected, not from the tennis team, but from the ball boy position because he was labeled "too clumsy." Smith didn't look back, though. He didn't allow himself to stay trapped in the past. He stayed focused on his dream and later won the US Open and many other major tennis tournaments.

Stan Smith

The Beatles. Few people can say they have never heard of this band. People still listen to their songs, and their hits playing on radios, movies, and iPhones around the world. But when they were young, a recording company told them their sound was "on its way out" and that no one would like guitar music anymore.

The Beatles

J.K. Rowling. From a cramped apartment, broke and raising her daughter on her own, Rowling went from twelve book rejections and an ongoing battle with depression to finally landing a deal with a publisher. Her Harry Potter books are currently the bestselling book series of all time, and the franchise has grossed over twenty-five billion dollars between books, movies, merchandise, and more.

J.K. Rowling

So, back to you. Your past? Yeah, it might not be great, but that's not an excuse. Failure and pain can show us our purpose. The things that have hurt us the deepest can show us our greatest passions. What you have tried to run from may be the thing that gives you purpose and passion. Our ability to endure hardship shows us how much we really care and reminds us why we keep going.

The Wright Brothers could have given up after they had to move from their hometown, leave their jobs, and endure multiple crashes. But that's not what they wanted. They cared too much about their dream of a workable aircraft. Michael Jordan could have quit when he was stuck on his high school's junior varsity team. But he didn't give up hope.

Can you imagine how many people told Henry Ford that his idea would never work? "Henry, you have already failed numerous times! Why do you think this will work? Give it up!" And now, all those naysayers' descendants are riding around in something Henry is responsible for popularizing.

The list goes on, but the names you'll hear about are only those who decided to keep trying. It's those people who didn't look back. It's those people who knew how to find passion amid their pain.

So, what will future historians write about you? Maybe you didn't have a great upbringing. But is that where your story will end? Are you going to accept that excuse? Maybe someone cheated you in a business deal or a relationship. Maybe someone close to you betrayed you. Is that the end of your story, or is it the beginning?

Add a comma to the story, and keep writing. Don't look back. Keep stepping.

WHAT WILL THEY SAY ABOUT YOU?

How do people perceive you? Have you ever stopped to think about that?

Let's pretend you have lived a full life. You are on your deathbed and have no regrets—a life well lived! What would people say about you? What did you accomplish? What really mattered?

Think about your goals. Think about your passions. Imagine

who you want to grow into during your lifetime. What future accomplishments are you hoping for? What are the must-do items on your bucket list?

Maybe there's a particular university you'd love to attend. Maybe you know you want to pursue a certain degree. Maybe you already know what field you'd like to work in and how you want to impact that field. Write it out. Spill your dream education and dream career onto the page as if they've already happened.

What about your personal life? Do you want to get married? Have children? Do you want to adopt or foster? Do you envision yourself surrounded by grandchildren someday? Write it out.

Now think about your hobbies. What are you passionate about doing in your spare time? Will those hobbies influence your future? Will they influence those around you? Write a few sentences about what you liked to do and why it mattered.

What do you wish people would say about your character? Who do you want to *be* at your core? Maybe you hope to be remembered for your kindness or your willingness to help people in need. Maybe you want to be known for your tenacity in solving problems. Maybe you want to be known as someone who entertained others, bringing joy through art or music. Maybe you want to be known as someone who was faithful with every task handed to them, whether big or small.

What made your life really matter? Most of us don't have every detail of our futures mapped out, but looking ahead helps us identify what deserves our focus and effort here and now. And we should probably add a note at the bottom of all our imaginary life summaries: subject to change without notice. That's because we grow and evolve and discover new things about ourselves all the time. That's a good thing!

It's never too soon to think about what you would want to be said about your life someday. You're making targets for an incredible future.

LOOKING BACK

BY LUKE LEZON

When examining our past, there is a substantial difference between where we look and why we look. We must remain vigilant while reminiscing. We tend to justify looking back with the intent to remember God's faithfulness, when, really, we are fixated on our failures.

As Paul wrote Philippians 3:12–14, he was incarcerated. He had every reason to look back on what had gone wrong in his life. Instead, he penned these words to the Philippians and powerfully pried at the reality of being perfected in Christ: "Not that I have already obtained all this, or have already arrived at my goal, but I press on to take hold of that for which Christ Jesus took hold of me. Brothers and sisters, I do not consider myself yet to have taken hold of it. But one thing I do: Forgetting what is behind and straining toward what is ahead, I press on toward the goal to win the prize for which God has called me heavenward in Christ Jesus."

Paul reminds us of what we fail to acknowledge—while I am not perfect, I press on toward being perfected, because Jesus has made me His own. He says, "I press *on*," meaning, I press forward. I move toward my future destination that Christ has prepared, rather than wallowing in past devastation. I forget what lies behind me, and strain forward to what lies ahead. I press *toward* the goal for the prize of the upward call of God in Christ Jesus.

I love that word *straining*. Straining *forward*. The Greek word that is translated into our English word *strain* also means "to extend, to stretch forward," and it carried a deep meaning for the original readers. It didn't mean you were casually reaching for your remote from your sofa, but that you were racing, exerting every muscle and nerve in your body, putting every effort from every fiber of your being toward Christ's call on your life.

Are you leaving behind what Christ saved you from and using every ounce of your strength to strain forward toward what He has called you to? If you try to stretch forward while looking back, you will miss your mark. Hebrews 12:1–2 says, "Let us throw off everything that hinders and the sin that so easily entangles. And let us run with perseverance the race marked out for us, fixing our eyes on Jesus, the pioneer and perfecter of faith."

Throw it off, look away, and fix your eyes on Jesus, the pioneer and perfecter of our faith. Nothing that hindered you before lays claim to your future, because when Jesus stretched His arms out on that cross and paid the price we couldn't, dying the death we deserved, He laid claim to your future and your destination. He is calling you. The prize isn't the destination that He brings you to, but the relationship that you have with Him. Nothing can take that away from you, so look forward, my friends. The sins that you cannot forget, God refuses to remember.

CHAPTER 6

CALLING AND COURAGE

CALEB

Every phase of our lives has a purpose. Sometimes it's hard to see the purpose. Or if we do see it, it feels so small, like it's not a *real* purpose. But in some way, large or small, every moment brings us an opportunity to live more aligned with what God has established in us.

When I think about those who have gone before me—biblical heroes, men and women who have altered history, and even people of great faith living today—something about these individuals draws me in. It's not their ability to be perfect. It's their willingness to be vulnerable. It's their willingness to make the most of each moment along their journeys.

The greatest dreamers know something about leveraging where they are and what they have in order to get to where they want to be, no matter how small their opportunities or few their resources seem at the time.

A mentor of mine, Gary, once told me about a concept called the "nexus point." I was sharing some frustrations with him. I felt like I didn't have the resources I needed in order to devote myself to The Alternative full time, and I didn't know how to make my dream work.

He took a long pause—he did that sometimes, like he was gathering all the wisdom from years past. "Caleb, have you ever heard of a nexus point?"

Umm . . .

"You are at a nexus point," he said to me.

Uh, okay? Thanks, Gary, but not helpful, since I have no idea what that means.

As he went on, he further explained that I was in a season of waiting, but this season wasn't *just* for waiting. It was for working too.

"It's this idea that God has a plan, yes," Gary said. "You and I both have a purpose, yes. But God wants to combine these two things, interweaving His power and plan with our efforts and passions—using your steps of obedience and His divine plan together. It's not just a 'works' thing, Caleb. It's a grace thing. God is letting you be a part of the plan He has built."

Whoa.

I've come to understand that these moments that make history, our nexus points, occur when our callings and gifts collide with God's plan for our lives. Our courage plus God's initiative gives birth to our destiny. This takes more than just trusting there's a good plan out there for us. We must embrace that plan—not just longing for what tomorrow holds and dreaming about better, more notable days, but really digging in deep with the opportunities we've been given right now.

This isn't easy. We may look around at our "right now" lives and ask ourselves a lot of questions. "How can God launch me into a life of real purpose if I'm spending my days in the kitchen of a fast food restaurant?" Or, "Why would God use me now? I'm just a student."

These questions may feel real and important, but really, they're excuses that mix up our thinking and discourage us. These questions lead us to believe that God doesn't want to use us right now. He wants to wait until tomorrow or the next day or a more distant someday when we're more important.

But that's simply not true.

I'm writing this chapter on my break between sending and receiving book shipments for my boss and taking my grandmother's car to the tire shop. That's my day today—emails, tires, and crafting words and ideas for this book. You see, God weaves great purpose and meaning into every day of our lives. Amid the mundane, we meet our purpose.

When we first started The Alternative in 2012, I closed four nights a week at a Chick-fil-A and mowed yards during the day while I finished my senior year of high school online. Austin had a lawn care business and was in college, commuting an hour to classes Monday through Friday.

There was no magical influx of cash coming in to help the ministry. We didn't even have a ton of free time to dedicate to it. God didn't audibly speak to us about the vision for this cause or what it might grow into years down the road. Right then, we just decided we needed to start a night of worship. It was a dream, and we embraced it with the small steps it took to

Embracing the plan, not knowing yet where it might lead

ORDINARY PERSON, EXTRAORDINARY PURPOSE

The people God often chooses to use are not the individuals who have it all together. They're not always people with a big title, a slick résumé, or a huge Instagram following. They're the people who were willing to say yes—people like you and me who are spending our days somewhere between mundane mediocrity and God-given purpose, people who are living in the middle ground.

Moses had to conquer the fear of failure. God, for some reason, chose a man who many believe had a speech impediment to be a mouthpiece for God's nation. I'm sure there were people who may have seemed more prepared, but God chose Moses.

God chose Abraham, an old man, to be the father to his nation. God chose Gideon, a man who was terrified, to be a military leader who went into battle against an entire army with only three hundred men. And he won. God met Gideon's extraordinary courage and obedience with victory, just like He wants to meet our obedience.

Think about this for a second. Even Jesus's mother Mary became pregnant with Jesus before she married Joseph. Imagine how confusing this must have been for her friends and family. But God still chose Mary for this task. He created her for this purpose.

God wants to use you right where you are, no matter how unqualified you may feel. We determine how much influence we will have tomorrow by deciding how available we will be to those around us today.

When we look back over history, it's easy to see how God used ordinary people in ordinary moments to do extraordinary things. But it's important to recognize the fingerprints of God in our today, not just our yesterday. Hindsight is clear. Looking back and understanding is easy. It doesn't require faith. It's fact.

Trusting that God is working now, in our mundane, every-day lives—that takes faith!

get there in the midst of our busy, very ordinary lives. Dreams take action. God blessed that.

DO SOMETHING ABOUT IT

Your greatest opportunity to embrace your purpose in life comes in the small moments. It's in the here and now that we prove to ourselves how much the dream matters. What others see as mundane, you can see as magnificent. Imagine what could be—what the future might hold—and work in the present to realize those visions.

You may not have much time in the day to dream, so steal any little moment you can. The late nights and early mornings are exhausting—press on. Let people hear the passion in your voice when you talk about something that hasn't happened yet. When you catch a glimpse of something new, something that's different, run with it. Your peers won't see the hours of work or the number of tears—they don't see the big picture like you do. They won't know how to measure this kind of work, but God most definitely does. He's been watching the entire time, and He sees every minute of your hard work.

These are the moments that will set you apart. These are the moments that will teach you and prepare you, reminding you that the greatest test of character is your ability to remain committed, even when your work feels unfulfilling, boring, or meaningless.

Every dreamer has this collision moment—a moment when the courage of a human is met by the calling of God. These moments don't always change our external circumstances, but they do reshape our perspectives. They are moments where pain is repurposed into a mission to heal others, moments where the struggle evolves into strength. What hurts us today often helps others tomorrow.

Some of the most powerful and effective communicators of hope are the people who have been hopeless before. Children who were adopted often have the greatest hearts for childcare facilities. Those who have been on the streets are often the first to champion the homeless. Our calling, our struggles, and our courage must all work together.

The repetition, the consistency, the endurance—meet it with resilience now. Moments where dreams and struggles meet God's calling are like the final few hundred feet on the runway when the plane finally gets lift and climbs, soaring above the earth. You may not have noticed, but planes don't always land on the same side of the runway. Sometimes they land in one direction, and on other days, they come from another angle. This is because planes have to take off into the wind.

It's not the speed of the plane or the power of the engines but the force of wind against the aircraft that lifts the plane and sends it soaring. The dreamer understands that soaring is not about avoiding resistance; it's about leveraging it. If there's no resistance, there will be no lift. Our engine and our struggles are what send us soaring.

We all want God to work through us. That's our greatest dream. And perhaps we imagine this as a glamorous, important job. But God can use us right where we are.

So, what's in your life today that you need to embrace? Maybe it's painful and doesn't make much sense. Perhaps it seems mundane and unimportant—only you know.

Just remember, God doesn't only meet us in our moments of victory and recognition. He loves to meet us in our everyday obedience. It's not about meeting Jesus one day. It's about walking with Him *every* day through the good, the bad, and everything in between. Embrace where you are. Take your gifts and passions, add God's purpose to the mix, and just watch what He will do.

CELEBRATE TODAY—PHOTO COLLAGE

Do you ever feel like there's nothing happening in your life that's worth noticing? It's a pretty normal feeling that we all experience sometimes, particularly when we're in the "in-between" phases of our lives.

But we know that these days matter to the big-picture plans unfolding moment by moment. Today matters because it's part of your story. So let's focus on appreciating today. Let's notice the small things.

In this era of social media, most of us are used to taking pictures. It's easy to pull out our cell phones and snap the perfect Instagram share. But we're going to take it in a different direction. We're going to take some pictures we *don't* plan to share.

That's right. These are just for you. As you move through your day, take at least ten pictures. Maybe that will include a selfie or two, but maybe not. Look for things, people, places, or moments to document that you might not normally notice. Find the beauty in those moments, and snap a picture.

It may take you a couple of tries to really get the hang of this. After all, the point isn't really the pictures. The point is about changing your mindset to notice that your mundane, regular life is filled with extraordinary beauty. All our lives are. Embrace the process.

Once you have a set of pictures, you can print them out,

download them to your computer, or just play around with them in an app. Create a collage, if you like, or maybe just make an album you can flip through. How does it feel to look back on those extraordinary, ordinary moments? Did you even realize you had so many of them in a typical day?

See if you can recognize the beauty in the ordinary. It's all part of God's plan for your life. Embrace it.

WHAT'S YOUR SCORECARD?

BY GRANT SKELDON

I used to spend so much time judging my life by the wrong scorecard.

I'd say to myself, "I thought by now I'd already be doing this or doing that."

I'd say to God, "Why does he get to do this? Why does she get to do that?"

God, when are You going to show me Your will for my life? And when am I going to get my big opportunity?

I was constantly judging my life by where I "should" be or where others were. It was a vicious cycle. And it was *never enough*, because it was a changing scorecard of things that were impossible to achieve and exhausting to strive for. Worse, I found out the hard way that the loneliest feeling in the world is when you finally achieve what you've made ultimate in your heart . . . and it doesn't actually *satisfy* you. In a lot of ways, when I was living in this struggle, I made God's plan more important than God Himself. I wanted His plan for my life more than I wanted Him.

In Ephesians 4:1, Paul urges us to "live a life worthy of the calling you have received."

Key word: *You* have been called.

I think a lot of us are missing our calling because we envy someone else's. I don't judge today by tomorrow anymore. I judge today . . . by today. And not other people's today. *My* today. Because all I can control is how I walk in *my* calling.

By the way, God doesn't tell us to run in our calling. Nope. He tells us to *walk*. Walking gives us time and presence to appreciate our surroundings. Just like exploring New York City—some people walk, but most people rush. They're *racing* through the day, on to the next thing. Everyone is in such a hurry! In the same way, a lot of us aren't enjoying today because we're running toward tomorrow. We've made our destination ultimate, and the journey is just an *obligation*.

Francis Chan said, "I think a lot of us need to forget about 'God's will for my life.' God cares more about our response to His Spirit's leading today, in this moment, than about what we intend to do next year. In fact, the decisions we make next year will be profoundly affected by the degree to which we submit to the Spirit right now, in today's decisions [...] To be honest, I believe part of the desire to 'know God's will for my life' is birthed in fear and results in paralysis."[1]

If you judge your life by *your* plans, then you're destined for disappointment.

Why? Because Christians never know the plan, *ever*.

Do you think the disciples knew the plan? No. They just followed Jesus day by day.

Do you think Mary knew the plan? No. She just listened to the Spirit day by day.

Do you think Moses knew the plan? No. He just followed God day by day.

Manna only lasted one day, and when the Israelites tried to plan around the next, it spoiled.

Have you ever noticed that God said He's a lamp to our feet, not a lighthouse to our path? He gives us enough light to see the next step. No farther.

So what if you stopped being dominated by the pressure of the future and just went all out with every opportunity and every person God put before you . . . today? Jesus said, "Can any one of you by worrying add a single hour to your life?" (Matthew 6:27). In fact, Jesus went on to tell us not to even "worry about tomorrow,

---

1   Francis Chan, *Forgotten God: Reversing Our Tragic Neglect of the Holy Spirit* (Colorado Springs: David C. Cook, 2009), 120.

for tomorrow will worry about itself" (Matthew 6:34).

Jesus was the only one who knew the full plan. He was the only one who knew *tomorrow*. And He said, *don't live there*. Don't worry about it. I'm convinced that we shouldn't be dominated by tomorrow but rather devoted to today. We shouldn't end our day asking ourselves, "Am I where I want to be?" We should end our day asking ourselves, "Was I faithful with today?"

That is now my scorecard. I encourage you to try it.

CHAPTER 7

GOD, DO IT AGAIN

AUSTIN

As we start to move forward in our lives, heading toward our dreams, we sometimes feel the urge to look back. This is a bad thing if we look back the way Lot's wife looked back (remember the pillar of salt in chapter 5?). But remembering where you have been is not always a negative thing; it can have a positive effect on where you are currently and where you plan on going in the future. Sometimes when we look back, it's so we can see how far we've come. What could be more motivating than to remember all the progress we've already made?

March 16, 2012, is a night I will never forget. It was a night when, for the first time, I asked myself, "Am I crazy for doing what I'm doing?"

Have you ever been there? I feel like most of us have been at some point. You get that feeling—like the steps you're taking are not comfortable at all. You don't know the outcome. You don't know how you'll get there or what it will even look like. You just know you're doing something different, and it's terrifying.

That's how I was feeling. It was the night of the first-ever Alternative gathering.

We had planned this event for months. As two broke college students, we were trying to figure out marketing ideas to get people to a new kind of event—a night of worship, where people could hear from God with no restraints, with no schedule for what time we had to start and what time we had to end.

We ordered flyers and started posting them all over town. We put a flyer in every Starbucks we could find (including the one I'm sitting in as I write this chapter).

After all the careful planning and extensive spreading of the word, the day for our event had come. We started setting up all the speakers, chairs, lights, and candles. It was a tad weird. We had no idea what we were doing, but we knew we were following a dream God wanted for us, and we were looking forward to seeing what God would do with our efforts.

We met on the basketball court in an old gym, where we had put a stage together for our speakers and band. We figured seven o'clock would be a good time for everyone, so we planned to start around then. We expected a good number of students from the local high schools and youth groups.

At 6:45, I finished talking with the band and making sure they had everything they needed. We were just about fifteen minutes from opening the doors when I peeked outside and saw maybe fifteen people standing outside under the awning.

I couldn't believe it.

I was shocked. Angry, even. In my mind, I started letting God have it.

I thought You called us to this. I expected to see more than fifteen people outside. What's going on?

A few more thoughts crossed my mind—ones I shouldn't write in this book. When I say I was angry, I mean I was really angry. I stormed to the back of the room. I grabbed Caleb and proceeded to share my frustrations with him.

We had worked so hard to plan this event. We'd invited so many people, put up so many flyers, and no one was there!

You have got to be kidding me.

We didn't know what to do, except talk to God. I remember praying with Caleb for a good five minutes. We prayed for God to humble us. We prayed to understand. We prayed, "God, if You want us to have fifteen people, let us give all the glory to You."

We ended the prayer and walked back inside. We gave the go ahead for the band to load onto the stage. I made my way to the front door and took a deep breath.

I opened the door to welcome everybody, and my heart stopped at what I saw. There were over a hundred people standing on that patio. Almost in tears, I started ushering people into the building, thanking them for coming and telling them how excited I was for them to be a part of the night.

That night was a start to something special for our community.

We carried on doing The Alternative for more than two years, watching as God did something big—bigger than we could have ever imagined. Churches that you would have never expected to come together were worshiping under the same roof to the same God. I'm so glad we didn't walk away at the first whisper of failure.

We outgrew many venues and saw hundreds come to find a relationship with God. Schools started seeing a difference in their classrooms, and parents were seeing their children act differently at home. It was a humbling time to be a part of something only God could do.

Around the fall of 2014, we started seeing our attendance decline every month. Soon, we realized there wasn't a hunger for God within the people who were attending or within our community. When we started The Alternative, there was a need in our community that no one was willing to help fill. We saw that need

One of the last The Alternatives before our break.

and tried to provide something meaningful, but the need wasn't there like it had been before.

We took a hard look at our lives. Caleb and I were burnt out and made the call to take a step back from doing an Alternative every month. It wasn't easy, but it for sure was necessary.

Even though it was a hard decision to make, the choice helped me learn more about my true self. My identity isn't in what I do; it's in who I am. And, ultimately, the decision to step away from The Alternative was only a temporary one.

THE SECOND CAST
LUKE 5

That first Alternative event brings to mind a story about Jesus and the disciples from Luke 5.

Jesus was in the boat of a fisherman who happened to be Simon Peter. Simon had just finished a long night of fishing and hadn't caught a single thing.

So we can guess that he was less than thrilled when Jesus told him to row out farther and put down his nets … again. Maybe Simon was even a little annoyed. He answered Jesus, "Master, we've worked hard all night and haven't caught anything." But Simon followed up with obedience: "But because you say so, I will let down the nets."

Want to guess what happened when they let down the nets? They caught so many fish that the nets began to break. They signaled to their friends to come help bring up the catch, and there were so many fish that both boats began to sink. (Don't worry, they didn't sink . . . they just ended up with *a lot* of fish.)

I love the moment when Jesus looked at Simon and told him to cast his nets back into the water. At that moment, Simon and his brother Andrew were tired. They had just finished up a full workday. They were cleaning their nets, getting ready to call it a night. They already had worked many hours with no results. But Jesus was clear: cast your nets back out.

Simon's response showed hesitation. He didn't want to go back out. When I imagine myself in Simon's shoes—or sandals, I guess—I wonder if he was thinking, *Are You crazy? We've been out all night and haven't caught a single fish!*

Then he moved past his hesitation and said, "But if You say . . ."

It is tough to get over the disappointment, anger, frustration, or weariness we feel when it seems like our efforts haven't produced the results we expected. It's not easy to feel the sting of what looks like failure and then hear, "Go do it again."

But look at what happened on the second cast. Look at what happened when Simon and Andrew obeyed and tried again, rather than throwing in the towel.

Is there a place in your life where God is asking you to throw out your nets for a second cast? Don't let discouragement get the best of you! Try again—throw down your nets, and see what kind of fish you pull up. You may be surprised.

DO SOMETHING ABOUT IT

How often is our first response hesitation? How often is something—a dream, a desire, a daring first step—whispered into our hearts, only to be smacked down by our negative thoughts?

No, I couldn't possibly do that. I've already tried, and it didn't work. Last time I chased a dream, I failed. I got hurt and discouraged, and I don't want to try again.

We all know those feelings. When I saw only fifteen people standing outside the door that first night, I wanted to give up before I'd even begun. But I needed two things: an attitude adjustment (fifteen people is fifteen lives that could be changed!) and the courage to recast my nets. So try again. Keep going, and don't give up on a dream because the first attempt didn't go as planned.

We go through our lives experiencing great times,

experiencing bad times, and sometimes facing challenges that were so difficult that we gave up. We didn't want to keep going. It was too tough. We weren't seeing any progress, so what was the point?

Maybe some of you have been praying for your parents or another family member or a friend, asking God to show Himself to them. Maybe you've been asking God to show Himself to *you* because you're not sure how real He is.

Maybe you're having troubles in relationships that are important to you—with family members or friends. Maybe you've tried to work through issues and find solutions, but it feels like you're not getting anywhere. You're tired, and you don't want to pour anything else into that relationship.

Or maybe it's the idea or dream God gave you years ago that never worked out, so you gave up. Maybe it's the business that couldn't get off the ground like you thought it would, so you scrapped the idea. Sometimes we abandon a calling, a dream, because we experience a little pushback. It's uncomfortable. We don't like that, so we run from the entire risky idea.

It's easy to look back on our mistakes and failures and let them overwhelm us. But instead, what if we challenge ourselves to be fueled by those past missteps—to consider them first attempts rather than last attempts? Keep hoping. Be fueled and encouraged, and go back after it again!

Do you feel a nudge in your soul right now? What's it saying?

It's time to go back again.

And maybe it is. Maybe it's time to attempt the dream that's stuck in your heart and won't let go—the one you think of every night as you fall asleep and when you wake up in the morning.

A year and half went by before I realized that my dream of

The Alternative could not be abandoned any longer. I was ready to see God revisit what He had started when The Alternative had been new. I was ready to recast my nets.

The Bible says God knew us before we were even formed in the womb (Jeremiah 1:5). He knows every cell in our bodies, every dream in our hearts. Are we willing to trust Him when He nudges us? Are we willing to believe in the dreams and ideas He has given to us?

Go back again. Recast your nets, and see what you pull up!

WHERE TO CAST YOUR NET

Grab your favorite journal (or note-taking app) and write down three to five dreams that have failed or stalled. Don't worry; I promise this won't be too depressing. Just jot them down—a handful of dreams or goals that didn't work out the way you had hoped they would.

Now take a second look at that list. Do you have enough distance from those letdowns to analyze them? Write some notes about each one if you can. Some of these dreams may be dreams God said no to. Maybe they weren't part of His plan because they weren't a good fit for you, long-term. Do you see any of those on your list? If so, draw a line through those to remind yourself not to look back at those ill-fitting dreams.

But perhaps others on your list deserve a second look. Maybe those dreams have stalled out because the timing wasn't right or you needed to grow into the fulfillment of that dream. Maybe you had some lessons to learn before you could fully embrace the vision. Do you see anything on that list where God might be saying, "Take another shot. Recast your net. See what you pull up"?

It takes practice to figure out when it's best to let go and when God wants us to lower our nets for a second try. That's why it's good to get into the habit of reassessing our plans—even those that didn't initially work out! See what insights you have when you take time to think through your stalled dream list, and pray about how God wants you to grow through this exercise.

Q&A WITH ADAM WEBER

Q: What's your story, and have you ever experienced a season of burnout?

A: Burnout can present in a lot of different ways, but my story of burnout went something like this: I became a pastor and started Embrace Church when I was twenty-four years old. It wasn't my idea. I was available, and God had a plan. We started with thirty-two people, and after six years, we became one of the fastest-growing churches in the country. I couldn't keep up with that kind of growth. One night, we had a leadership meeting at the church. Someone asked me how I was doing, and I just started sobbing. I was burned out. Looking back, I realize I was leading and pastoring a church completely on my own strength and abilities. My life, words, actions, relationships, and even my soul showed it. I couldn't do it anymore.

Q: How did you make it out of that season and get healthy again after burnout?

A: I'm not a counselor or psychologist, but here are some of the things that helped me get out of my season of burnout:

- Turn off your phone. It can be hard to put down your phone. (Trust me, I know.) Try intentionally checking it a few times after work instead of habitually checking it every three seconds.
- See a counselor. Find a Christian counselor that you can be real and honest with, and go see them at least once every other month.

- Practice Sabbath. I don't have an off switch, so this is one of the hardest commandments in the Bible for someone like me to keep. It's important to take a day away from work to do what makes your soul feel refreshed.
- Take care of yourself! Watch what you eat. On a regular basis, find time to go on a walk or run. Also, get some sleep! Put your phone down and go to bed.

Q: *Where is God's heart on burnout?*

A: God tells us that we get burned out for two reasons: we forsake Him, and we try to do things on our own. Basically, we're trying to carry something we were never meant to carry. God doesn't want us to be burned out. He wants us to depend on Him, and that all starts with allowing Him to be the true Lord of our lives.

Q: *The story of Andrew and Peter casting their nets a second time shows us what it looks like to be obedient to God, even when we don't think He will deliver. Why is it important to trust God in all circumstances?*

A: Jesus calls us to be obedient, even when we can't see the end result. Sometimes that requires blind trust, just saying, "God, I've done everything I can. Now I trust Your plan for this situation." This is hard, especially when the circumstance makes it seem like trusting God is the last thing you should do. But I've seen God come through in some impossible situations, and I know He will again, every time.

CHAPTER 8

REMEMBER THE PROMISE

CALEB

Do you ever wake up and feel like you're living the dream? Some days are like that. I can recall many in my life—beautiful days, full of joy and happiness. Moments when I recognized how amazing life is. Moments when God came through. Prayers were answered. Hard work was rewarded. Everything was unfolding just as I'd hoped. In these moments, you feel like you are soaring.

But then there are days when your dream feels more like a nightmare. The days when you think you're on the right path, trying to make good choices, but everything feels like it's falling apart. Maybe people you were close to decide to walk away. Or you've been praying with all your heart, only to hear a big *No* from God. Or you make a foolish decision and experience harsh consequences because of it.

Ouch.

These times are painful. I don't think anyone likes to go through a season like that, and yet we all do. Want to know what I've learned? Every moment—even the nightmares where your heart is in pieces—is part of the journey. Remember David in the field, the shepherd boy? Remember the lion he fought off? He must have been scared in that moment, but that trial prepared him for his future. Our temporary trials are what strengthen us too.

You've heard about some of the first Alternative events. You've heard about how the idea started. You've heard about my dreaming spirit and Austin's beautiful baby girl. It's easy to make a God journey sound like it's constantly exciting and fulfilling. We focus on those awesome high points where God showed up because those stories are powerful!

But when we tell about those exciting moments, it's easy to overlook the whole story. It's easy to drown out the struggle with the highlights. And we love to do that, don't we? But I want to share some of those days that didn't feel like a dream. I want to share some of the days that felt like a nightmare, because I want you to know that struggles don't mean God isn't with you. They just mean He's worth it.

I remember the first event we did in a facility that we had never been in before. This was our sixth or seventh event overall, back in 2013. We set off the fire alarm before the event even started because we ran our fog machine too long. The fire marshal showed up—the fire truck, the whole deal—all while I was trying to prepare to preach that night.

But wait, it gets worse. Way worse.

Early on, Nick, a big mentor in my life, gave us several hundred dollars so we could create some small invite cards. We had them printed the day before the event and took them to the local high school football game to hand out and place on cars. Awesome, right? Except the month was printed wrong on the cards. Completely wrong date.

Oh, there's more.

One of the most embarrassing things we ever did was when we had a misspelling printed on a shirt. We somehow missed a typo on the T-shirt proof and had *Actuvity* rather than *Activity* printed on five hundred shirts. Super professional.

These trials were self-inflicted, and we can look back on them and laugh now. But that's not true of all the hard days on our journey.

Leadership can get extremely lonely, especially when you are a young, single leader. I remember a day, several years back, when Austin called me. We were both super frustrated—hurt more than anything. It was two o'clock in the morning. We had been let down by a couple of people close to us. We were beaten down by constantly hearing their complaints about what we weren't doing and how we could be better. It hurt us both so badly that we had to do something about it. We decided we were going to go to Walmart, purchase thank-you cards, and write every person on our team a personal note in appreciation of something they had done over the past year. This wasn't some quick attempt to win back everyone's favor. We wanted to fight off the hurt with gratitude. And we did.

Leadership can be a lonely place.

I remember the third time I preached. I had prepared the message for a few months and was so excited—and really nervous—to share it. I got up, preached, and people responded well.

But, even so, as I walked off the stage and behind the curtain, negative thoughts overtook me.

I didn't do good. I could have said that better.

Feelings of inadequacy swept over me. I was afraid to even walk back on stage.

I know that person will disagree with what I am saying.

There have been times I have walked off the stage and wanted to cry because I tried to give it everything I had and felt like I missed the mark. I feel like that a lot, honestly. There's a constant sense that I can do better.

Recently, I have had to overcome deeper and more personal issues. In a matter of six months, I lost a grandfather who I was very close to, a relationship fell apart, and I started another ministry. I had an uncle who died within three months of moving into my house and getting put on hospice care. I've been working

My father and grandfather

to keep watch on a very close friend struggling with suicidal thoughts.

I've been trying to manage all this personal stuff while trying to "dream big."

Has your life ever looked like that? I know I'm not alone.

At times, I wondered if everyone was going to walk out on me, if anyone really understood me. At times, I felt like people adored me from a distance but didn't care to know me up close … like they only wanted my attention because they were curious about me.

Being known doesn't replace that desire we all have to feel *valued*. Really, it only makes things worse. Being in the spotlight doesn't fix your issues, it just makes them more noticeable. I learned that the hard way. "You will burn faster in the spotlight," my friend Tyler Dunn has always reminded me.

Some of the loneliest times in my life weren't the days of being unknown, but the nights after our biggest events—after giving it everything I had, after praying with people and pouring my heart out. The nights after seeing God move so radically in the lives of hundreds of people, and praying He could do the same in mine.

It was in these moments of brokenness that God taught me a beautiful lesson.

One February night in 2017, I had just gotten back from a work trip. At the time, I was doing some creative design for a well-known fast food restaurant. They had held a large conference that had me out of town for four days. I got back late on a Tuesday night and was welcomed by a cluster of problems. I decided to go for a run that night and ended up pacing back and forth on a quiet little road about a mile from our house. I was flooded with fear and anxiety. What was I supposed to do? How could I fix everything?

And God wasn't helping.

God, how can I fix this? What can I say?

What about these people . . . will they ever change?

Nothing.

God! I'll do anything. I just need a direction . . .

So much was happening in my life at once. It was a time of acceleration, and all I wanted was for God to give me some action steps. You know, like a to-do list, or a road map.

But He never did.

I walked home that night. As the hours ticked by, I found peace in remembering who God had been to me over years. I thought about the times when I needed Him, and how He was there. I thought about the times when people tried to accuse me, and He stood by my side. I thought about the times when the enemy came after me, and He protected me. I thought about the times I royally screwed up, and He still chose me. I thought about the times I had been hurt, and He healed me. I thought about the nights I had been betrayed, and He comforted me. I thought about the times I had been broken, and He held me. I thought about the people who had broken their promises to me, and He still kept His. Thank you, God.

I decided in that moment not to look for a supernatural sign that everything was going to be okay, but just to remember who my God was. Faithful and true. Steadfast. Constant. The God of Jeremiah was my God too. Wow. A promise-keeping God! And that's where I put my trust—in remembering who He was. A promise maker, and a promise keeper.

JEREMIAH'S PROMISE-KEEPING GOD
BOOK OF LAMENTATIONS

When it looks like defeat is near, it's hard to remember God's promises.

Jeremiah knew what this felt like. When he felt defeated, he took to pen and paper to write about it—words we can read today in the book of Lamentations. Because of how vivid his writings are, many scholars believe he was writing his thoughts amidst the rubble of an overtaken Jerusalem. As ash filled his lungs and the scent of death overwhelmed him, he began to write what we now know as Lamentations 3. Writing was all he knew to do in his brokenness.

It was 586 BC, and Jerusalem had just been sieged. The people had been slaughtered and burned, some crushed by the rubble. Some had been taken into captivity in Babylon. The wall had been destroyed. This was a bad day, to say the least.

And in the midst of this, Jeremiah began to write. Look at these words from Lamentations 3:1–6:

> I am the man who has seen affliction
> by the rod of the LORD's wrath.
> He has driven me away and made me walk
> in darkness rather than light;
> indeed, he has turned his hand against me
> again and again, all day long.
> He has made my skin and my flesh grow old
> and has broken my bones.
> He has besieged me and surrounded me

with bitterness and hardship.
He has made me dwell in darkness
like those long dead.

The cries of Jeremiah go on for several more verses. Can you relate to his desperation? I know I can. In fact, I think *everyone* can relate because we are humans, and these are human feelings. Feeling betrayed, forgotten. Or maybe you feel hurt, more than anything. You are sitting in the dust and the mess of a "Did that really just happen?" moment. That's where Jeremiah, mighty prophet of God, was too.

He was mentally and spiritually confused. See, he *knew* in his mind that God was going to do something special in this place. Something miraculous, even. Because that's what God does. But . . . how? How could God show up in such a broken place at such a bad time? It's in the middle of defeat and despair that God often meets us. We ask:

"Where are you, God?"

"What are you doing?"

"This makes no sense . . ."

"You were supposed to come through this time!"

We can look back and read what happened after Jeremiah's "But how, God?" moment. We can see how God redeemed His people from captivity. We know Jerusalem was rebuilt. The wall was restored. And Jesus came afterward for the spiritual redemption of the world. God remained faithful to His promises, both to Jeremiah and to His people.

That promise-keeping God is the same God who is with us today.

DO SOMETHING ABOUT IT

I don't know what you're up against. You might be reading this book in a hospital bed fighting for your life. Maybe you're reading it in your room, the only place you feel like you can be yourself. Maybe you're reading it in the middle of the worst breakup of your life. Maybe you're in the car headed somewhere you dread. I don't know your story, but God does, and He has a promise for you. A personal promise. A promise so intimate, it can give you peace in your darkest moments and rest when the tension is high. That's the power of a promise from God.

No matter what you face, remember the God you serve, and remember His promises—because your circumstances should never determine your faith. Faith does not come from circumstances; we have faith despite our circumstances.

No matter what you face, remember the God you serve, and remember His promises.

Throughout this past year, I have journaled some promises I have found in God's Word. I pray these will bring you hope as you continue pressing forward on the path of great resistance.

He gives us firm steps. (Psalm 37:23)
We can have an eternity with Him. (John 3:16)
He is our comforter. (Psalm 46)
He is our guide. (Psalm 23)
He is our savior. (Jude 20–25)
He is our forgiver. (Ephesians 4:32)
He is our lover. (Deuteronomy 7:7–14)
He is our strength. (Psalm 28)
Dry seasons are not dead seasons. (Ecclesiastes 3:1–14)

He never sleeps. (Psalm 121:3–4)
He has not forgotten about us. (Matthew 28:16–20)
He is with us. (Deuteronomy 31:6–8)
He sees us. (Genesis 16:13)
He will not betray us. (Psalm 89:1–8)
He will not let us fall too far. (Psalm 121)
He is our provider. (Matthew 6:25–34)
He is our healer. (James 5:13–16)
He has numbered my days but not numbered my soul
because I am His masterpiece. (Psalm 139:16)
He sees my pain. (Psalm 34)
He knows what I care about. (Psalm 38:9)
My suffering is not wasted. (Romans 8:18–39)
He is still on plan A. (Isaiah 41)
We are not an accident. (Psalm 139:13–18)
God is with me, and He is with you. (1 Corinthians 3:16)

Do any of these promises speak to you right now? Even though I'm past many of the crises that inspired this list, these promises still speak to me. You don't have to be in a dark place to be encouraged by these reminders.

But maybe you are in a dark place right now. Maybe you're in that place where what you know in your heart—that God is good and that He has a plan for you—doesn't line up with what you see with your eyes.

It's like when you are watching a sick family member get sicker, or a friendship plummet.

Trusting God during the mess is the full truth of a faith-based life. Because if you could *see* hope, it would not be true hope. It would just be sight. Living in hope doesn't always mean you will have a clear vision—just a firm calling.

When we read further into Jeremiah's writings in Lamentations 3:21–26, his tone changes:

Yet this I call to mind
and therefore I have hope:
Because of the LORD's great love we are not consumed,
for his compassions never fail.
They are new every morning;
great is your faithfulness.
I say to myself, "The LORD is my portion;
therefore I will wait for him."
The LORD is good to those whose hope is in him,
to the one who seeks him;
it is good to wait quietly
for the salvation of the LORD.

What changed for the author when he chose to "call to mind"? Visibly, nothing. The Babylonians had still invaded. People were not rising from the dead, and the city was not magically reassembled. In fact, during the period he spent writing this, it's possible that even more people suffered and died. If nothing is changing, why is the author suddenly so understanding of God's goodness? Why is he no longer doubtful? Why isn't he questioning God's ways anymore? How is he okay with everything going on around him?

It's simple—he remembered God's character. He remembered God's promises. He could stand in the middle of this nightmare because he knew this wasn't the end. This was the beginning of the next phase, and he knew God would finish what He started.

The trial you're facing right now—or might be facing in the future—is not the end. It's just the beginning.

The trial you're facing right now—or might be facing in the future—is not the end. It's just the beginning—a new season of growth, the next step in maturity, and a new lesson in perseverance.

We must hold on to our vision and to our hope. We have to walk in faith, and faith means believing that our best days are not being left in the past.

Jeremiah kept hoping, kept believing, kept going. He was tenacious. Tenacity is a continued perseverance, and seeing our big dreams come to fruition requires Jeremiah-level tenacity sometimes.

Jeremiah wasn't oblivious to what was happening around him. He felt the destruction and the despair of his city. He wasn't careless. He just knew he had only one option—to trust that God is who He says He is.

Sometimes what seems to be a buried dream is just a planted seed that needs to root deeper. Is that your current situation? God will often plant the seeds of hope in the soil of great sorrow. In those times, remember that God is not burying you; He is planting you. It's in this soil, these bad circumstances, that we must continue to trust that God is moving and working.

It's time to stop counting yourself out. It's time to stop selling short what God is doing in your life. He has *not* left you. You are being prepared, planted, trained, purified. Maybe you're being protected.

Here's a truth that's tough to understand sometimes: God cares more about giving us joy than taking away pain. We can have joy despite pain. In fact, sometimes the only way to teach us about lasting joy that isn't dependent on our circumstances is by taking us through a valley of temporary pain.

So, when you don't know what to do, look back at who God has been. Remember His promises. Your pain is a massive opportunity to plant seeds of hope in the character of an unwavering and unchanging God.

REMEMBER WHAT HE HAS DONE—JOURNALING

Take a few minutes to write out all the times God has come through for you. There is nothing complicated or overly animated about this. It's important though.

So often, we beg for God to come through or to sustain us, and when He does, we forget. When we face our next trial, we allow anxiety to overtake us, sure we'll be swallowed up this time.

And what about all the times God came through in ways we didn't expect? Stuff might not have worked out the way we originally thought it would, but we're still left standing. God still sustained us. He's still with you when you face all your trials.

Now go ahead, remember all the times He has been faithful. Write out your own Lamentations 3, just like Jeremiah. It's okay if you're upset or frustrated. God knows that. Tell Him how you feel. Just try to point your writing toward what God has done for you, even if it doesn't all make sense.

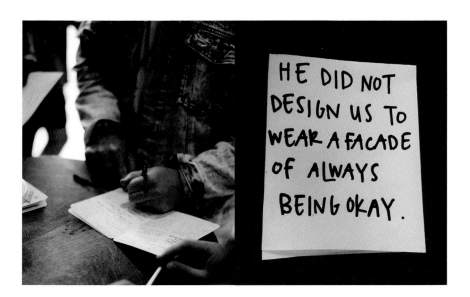

HE DID NOT DESIGN US TO WEAR A FACADE OF ALWAYS BEING OKAY.

MOURN IT AND MOVE ON

BY JOSH RHYE

Moving on is so much easier said than done. It's hard when someone breaks your heart, a friend betrays you, or you lose a loved one. When your heart is broken, it affects your appetite and ability to see life through the right lens. You begin to think you're broken or damaged goods because someone else can't see your value. My goal is to challenge your perspective and remind you that moving on is okay. In 2 Samuel, chapter 12, David fasted for seven days and refused to eat, begging God to spare his son. Once he realized his son had passed, he got up, worshiped God, and began a process of moving on. Moving on seems impossible when you're miserable, and as hard as that chapter is to read, I want us to see the importance of mourning loss and moving on.

The first funeral I ever preached at was for my youngest brother, Justin. Our family faced dark days of doubt, confusion, and loneliness. It's hard when you can call a person's cell phone but no one answers. When you can still see their Facebook profile but its feed is now filled with messages about resting in peace. My wife, church, kids, and best friends could never understand where my mind was during those days, but God did. He spoke to me like a friend and guided me like a Shepherd, reminding me of the power of Psalm 23. He led me through my ups and downs and through moments that would make you blush if you knew the whole story. But in the midst of it all, He was there, leading me and teaching me that it's okay to mourn . . . just don't dwell there. You must say to yourself, "I will dwell in the house of the Lord, not in a constant state of depression," knowing that letting go is part of allowing God to lead you.

You see, in the middle of mourning and moving on is a

miserable land where dreams and ministries die. It's hard to let people go, but the miracle is on the other side of moving on. Moses moved on from Egyptian bondage, and God parted the Red Sea. Joshua moved on and into the promised land after losing battles and best friends. David moved on after moral failure and penned songs we still sing today. Peter moved on after cussing Jesus and was the keynote speaker at Pentecost. Saul moved on and became Paul, the greatest missionary to ever live. Job moved on after losing everything, and God doubled his fortunes. Jesus was betrayed by His friend Judas and crucified by the church, but that didn't stop Him from completing His journey. He moved past death and purchased the miracle called salvation.

The devil wants you to believe your life, ministry, and relationships are dead and will stay in that tomb, but your third day is coming. God will give you the power to move on. Every promise needs some tomb time. Those dark hours teach us to trust God when we can't see a way out. So, take the time to mourn the loss, then move on. Your miracle is waiting.

CHAPTER 9

IF THEY ONLY KNEW

CALEB

Twelve hours. Twelve hours was all we had. Luke Lezon, Carson Case, and I were making a one-day trip to Los Angeles and back. We had everything planned: rental cars, travel routes, departure times, and arrival times. We had only a short window to accomplish all our goals because the very next day was an Alternative event.

After catching our early flight, getting our rental car, and arriving at our meeting, our day was on track. But we had no room for error. We all had agreed we would leave shortly after lunch. We *had* to leave then to catch our flight.

Lunch came, and our meeting drew to a close. Then a pastor offered a suggestion before everyone left: "How about we go around the room and pray for everything coming up?"

Now, don't get me wrong. I love prayer, but I have to admit, I wasn't thrilled. I didn't want to miss my flight. Not just any flight—the *last* flight to make it back home before The Alternative started.

This is not good, I thought.

Great meeting. Too bad we had a flight to catch . . .

As we pulled up to the airport, I took a few final sips from my water bottle and set it in my lap. Because I was in such a rush, I forgot to screw the lid back on. As I stood up out of our car, the water spilled all over my pants.

Great.

Just to be clear, it looked like I hadn't quite made it to the restroom. This was a disaster for my light denim jeans. We parked the car and dashed toward security. "Excuse me . . . coming through, excuse me."

As soon as we got to security, I heard the dreaded words no passenger wants to hear.

"Delta Flight 1720. Case, Lezon, Stanley. This is your final boarding call."

I bolted. This was no brisk walk: I was backpack-bouncing sprinting to the gate. This was like something straight out of *Mission: Impossible.*

I could practically hear the thoughts of everyone around me as they saw my pants. And my horror-painted face surely told on me. *These people think I'm running to the restroom a little too late.* But I had no time to change. There wasn't even time to breathe.

Man. If these people only knew what I've been through. If they only knew how my day started. If they only knew this was just water.

If they only knew . . .

Everybody has something. You may not have a crazy story about sprinting through an airport terminal, but if you are anything like me, I'm sure there have been times you have whispered to yourself, *If they only knew.*

We often use these four powerful words to justify why we behave the way we do. As I said those words under my breath, it gave me this strange sense of peace. I felt like I had a reason to be in the situation I was in, but no one else understood it. No one else could see it. There was a legitimate reason, if they only knew.

In this case, it's funny to look back on that moment. But

Home, and ready for the next Alternative gathering.

isn't this type of frustration and justification also the way it is with serious topics in our lives sometimes? We all have that thing we struggle with, and it's much bigger than a simple water bottle spill that would dry on the flight home.

Perhaps your struggles are internal—the insecurity that

haunts you in big crowds or the battles you fight to find your place in your circle of friends. Maybe it's your need for acceptance or approval. Maybe it's lust. Maybe it's the pain of a past relationship or the longing to feel loved and valued. *Will I ever get past this?* you wonder. *Am I even cared for? Am I needed? If they only knew how I feel.*

People may see a mess on the outside, but they have no idea what you have been through. They have no idea what's gotten you to that point.

Some of you reading this have felt judged your entire life because of your individual quirks, because of how you dress, or even because of your weight. *If they only knew,* you often think. *I didn't choose this.* This is a scary place to be when we all want to be seen and known. Loneliness and isolation can overwhelm us. They can push us away from community. *I want to be known . . . but if they only knew.*

I remember early in 2017, when everything was picking up for The Alternative, Austin and I would often end our conversations with comments like, "If they only knew . . ." If they only knew we didn't have the money to fund our venue next week. If they only knew Austin was working from seven o'clock in the morning until late into the night at a warehouse to provide for his family. If they only knew the opposition and spiritual warfare that came with our position at the helm of a growing ministry. If they only knew we didn't really know what we were doing. If they only knew . . .

But then my thinking began to change. I realized that someone did know.

NAAMAN: WEARING THE STRONGMAN SUIT
2 KINGS 5

We like to think our struggles are brand-new or unique to us. But we aren't the first to say, "If they only knew . . ." We aren't the only ones who feel isolated by our private truths.

In 2 Kings, there was a warrior named Naaman. Naaman was a leader in the Aram army. Strong and mighty, he was looked up to by the nation. He was a victor! He spent his days encouraging the army. He was the kind of man ladies would have loved. And he was the kind of man that men followed.

From the outside, this guy was set. Winning battles, gaining fame—the spotlight looked great on Naaman. But Naaman fought another battle—a private one. He defeated nations, but there was still something defeating him.

Naaman had leprosy, a disease that was literally eating his skin away. If people found out, he could be sent away forever. Leprosy was no joke. This was serious. The infection would start as blisters and eventually would lead to the loss of limbs. There was nothing Naaman could do to stop it. When he would shut the door to his room and begin to strip away the layers of his uniform, he would also peel back layers of skin. If people only knew what he was going through. The helmet and the armor covered his pain well. He looked strong, but his flesh was rotting.

Slowly deteriorating, Naaman must have been scared. Maybe this is why he had so much courage on the battlefield. Those fights were nothing compared to what he fought on the inside.

That wasn't the end of Naaman's story. God was gracious and healed Naaman, but it took Naaman being honest and vulnerable first. Admitting he wasn't strong enough on his own was what led to Naaman's redemption. Just like he did with Naaman, God sees our brokenness. We can't hide our struggles forever. But when we're willing to be honest with God, ourselves, and others, we live out the kind of authentic faith that brings people closer to Him. We build the kind of community we all long for.

DO SOMETHING ABOUT IT

Even though we may feel lonely, even though struggles may be strong and present in our day-to-day life, even though the prayers prayed and the tears cried in private won't be heard or seen by the world, our God sees them. It may feel like we are losing and just can't keep going, but our God hasn't walked out.

The scriptures tell us and show us that our God is the beginning and the end, that He is always present, and that He is with us. We can rest assured that no matter what we face, our God sees it. Our God has His eyes on us in the dark of the night and the light of the day. In your greatest victory, God is there! In your biggest mistake, He is still there. Maybe your friends have left you, you got turned down, you've made some dumb decisions—maybe you're feeling really defeated. But our God knows exactly what we are going through.

Maybe in those dark moments, the idea of God seeing

> We can rest assured that no matter what we face, our God sees it.

everything isn't even comforting. You don't want Him to know just how bad it is.

Don't be scared. We shouldn't fear being seen by God. God doesn't see and run. He sees and stays. He doesn't love you because of what you have done; He loves you *despite* what you have done. He loves us as much in our moments of crushing defeat as He does in our moments of greatest victory. His love is not acquired by mighty efforts. It's available all the time, to all people, no matter who we are, what we've done, or what we're struggling with. God sees it, and He stays, ready to help us if we'll ask.

What are you facing today? God sees it.

"If they only knew how lonely I felt." God knows.

"If they only knew how hard I struggled in my past relationships." God knows.

"If they only knew I was addicted." God knows.

"If they only knew . . ." God knows!

Think about who you believe God to be for a moment. We either live for a blind Father, following and worshiping someone who can't see or know us fully, or we serve a Father who sees right where we are, even now. This changes everything for us.

Suddenly, every aspect of our lives becomes clearer. The need to compete—to prove ourselves worthy of acclaim and affection—drifts away as we realize we are seen and loved, just as we are. Right now! God sees you and accepts you. The secret pain we endure alone becomes a shared burden with the God who sees, understands, and shoulders the load with us.

How can we forgive those who have hurt us? There is a God who sees us—who knows about every time we've failed and needed forgiveness, and who also sees how deeply we've been wounded by others. He gives us the strength to show grace to others in their failures.

How can we let stress and anxiety go? We have a God who

sees how much we struggle—a God who doesn't condemn us for our weaknesses but comes alongside us to lend *His* strength. We have a God who sees all of us.

I remember a time I visited a close friend in the hospital. This individual didn't have any family nearby. He was older than me, in his mid-forties. I had met him several years before, when I was helping pastor the church in LaGrange. I'll never forget the words he said to me in his hospital bed. He had almost lost his life the night before because of an infection in his lungs that came out of nowhere. His heart had actually stopped for a moment, but he was still alive and much more stable by the time I stopped by.

I asked him if he had told our old pastor how serious his condition was. "No," he said, "I'm scared to tell them about everything I am going through. I don't want to be a burden."

Wow. Oftentimes we hide our hurt and try to handle it on our own because we don't want to be vulnerable with God or others. But what if the pain in our lives is God's way of pulling us into a deeper, more sincere love? What if it's His way of giving us a platform?

What if our private struggles could be leveraged through vulnerability to bring people together and to share hope? People are not encouraged by our strength. They may be impressed, but they are not encouraged. They find hope through the times when we admit how weak we are. In those moments, we can all look around and say, "Wait, you too?"

The pain you experience can be a platform for those around you to see how much you really believe in God.

Nobody knows the full cost of the calling on your heart. Nobody knows what you have to deal with behind closed doors, but that's okay because God does.

He's not only there with us in public or present only in those mountain moments. He's a God who sees and knows—and stays with us—in the dark moments too. Rest in that truth.

TALK ABOUT IT

Sin grows in the dark. Whatever it is you're struggling with, I want to challenge you to bring it to the light. Maybe the sin you need to bring to light is something you're currently doing, but maybe it's something that happened in the past. We were not designed to carry the weight of this world on our own.

Think of a person with whom you can trust your heart. A mentor or a leader is a great option because they can usually provide good counsel if you need advice. But this could be a close friend or family member too. Ask this trusted person to pray for you. Tell them what you're struggling with now, or share that secret from the past you've been carrying around for so long.

This may be a challenge. It might be embarrassing. But just remember, the longer we hide our pain, the harder it is to confess our struggles and the more the weight of shame eats at us.

WHAT THEY DIDN'T KNOW

BY CHELSEA CROCKETT

There was a period in my life when I was dead set on moving to California and going to school there. So, my dad and I set out on a road trip from Illinois to the West Coast, and I started attending California Baptist University. The school was *amazing*, and the food was even better. Plus, the first week, we had what they called "Christian raves" for the freshmen, and whew, I was bumpin' when Lecrae trap remixes came on. I was meeting so many great people from all over and growing an appreciation for a different part of the country. (There are legit people in California who go surfing every weekend.)

Nearly all my friends back home had gone to the nearby university in Illinois, and a couple of them moved away, but we were communicating every other day. At the time, I was also in a dating relationship with a guy from home. We had no set plans for what direction we wanted to take things, which made me nervous because I liked him a lot at the time. I didn't realize it in the moment, but the relationship was unhealthy for many reasons. About three weeks into school, I went to a church service and audibly heard the voice of God call me out of that relationship. Immediately, my heart dropped. I was so confused. I tried to dismiss the voice and say it was my own voice, but as the day went on, God made it clear that it was Him.

That night, I couldn't sleep. I knew I needed to obey God, but my flesh didn't want to.

Meanwhile, I was getting used to being away from home, my family, and my dogs. I was taking six classes, keeping up with a regular posting schedule on my YouTube channel, and making friends. But at the same time, I couldn't keep down any food.

I had major depressive thoughts. And all I was thinking about during class was what God had said, and how my desires were completely the opposite. It got to the point where all I was doing was staying in my dorm, starving myself (because I didn't want to deal with it coming back up), and wrestling with the thoughts in my head. I was also dealing with major comparison issues with other girls. I was in a vulnerable place in my life for the enemy to whisper lies that were the opposite of who God says I am.

Four weeks in, right before the weekend hit, I couldn't deal with it anymore. I bought a plane ticket and went home for the weekend. I ended up following through with the breakup, even though I didn't want to at the time. I also decided to take a break from school.

Sadly, the depression didn't leave, and it's still something I battle with, off and on. As soon as I left, I received comments across my social media saying hateful things about me leaving the school. Some comments were from people I'd thought were good friends. If they only knew . . . maybe they would be more understanding.

Maybe your life looks a bit like my freshman year of college. Hope may feel a million miles away, and no one may seem to understand you or your situation. The one thing that I've learned is to embrace the hurt and not to run from it. Cry out to God, who is near even when it may not "feel" like it. Then cry out, again and again. He is listening, and He understands more than anyone on this earth ever will.

CHAPTER 10

WHO AM I

CALEB

"So how is The Alternative doing?" people began to ask me.

The question drained me every time I heard it. It wasn't because things were bad for The Alternative; it was because they were great, but I was exhausted. I wanted to say, "I have twenty-seven texts I haven't responded to yet concerning things that need to happen for The Alternative. Ask me something different, because I don't want to talk about The Alternative."

I was giving this dream everything I had, battling the tension of growth and trying to make something that would last. I loved what we were building, but I wanted someone to care about how *I* was, not just some brand called The Alternative. After all, a lot of people know The Alternative. But do they really know who I am?

I remember after The Alternative really took off in 2017, my normal was changing. What we were doing was becoming more and more public; it was the talk of the community. People had their opinions—good and bad.

In the past, I never saw myself as an introvert. I always thought I was someone who wanted to entertain the party, to

The stage only magnifies what happens in private.

socialize and engage with everyone. But I started to dread going places where everyone might know me. Socially, I was weary. I felt like everyone wanted something from me, but I just didn't have anything to offer. After all, who was I? What did I have to give that they couldn't get elsewhere? I'm just some kid who used to mow yards and clean toilets.

One night, I showed up at a friend's wedding reception in the area. After catching up with several people and, yes, telling them about "how The Alternative was doing," I sat back and caught up on my dinner. I remember eating a pasta dish with a Caesar salad and sitting at the far end of the table. A close friend's mother, Mrs. Elise Kilgore, came over to our table as I finished my meal. She's like a second mother to me, and I've always trusted her family.

"Caleb, do you mind if I tell you something?" she asked with great hesitation in her voice.

Mrs. Elise's son Josh is one of my best friends. We grew up

playing in the creek and pretending we were Navy Seals in the tree houses we would attempt to build in their backyard. From paintball wars to high school breakups, this family was my family. I always valued Mrs. Elise's words because I knew she had my best interests in mind, and more than anything, I knew she knew me. *Me*, not my brand.

"Yes, please do! Tell me," I said eagerly.

I didn't know what it was yet, but the look on her face and the tone of her voice told me that she understood something many did not. It was that whole "If they only knew . . ." thing, but in reverse. It was like she could see something about me, something I didn't quite understand myself. I trusted what she was going to say before even hearing it. I leaned in . . .

"Being in the position you are in can be really lonely," she said. "I've seen it for some time now and was waiting for the right moment to tell you. I just want you to know that you will always be Caleb to our family."

Those words almost had me crying at a dinner table in public.

Now, you might be thinking, "What's the big deal? Of course you'll always be Caleb. Isn't that your name?"

But what Mrs. Elise said was something I'd needed to hear for a long time. Her words reminded me who I was. I wasn't Caleb from The Alternative. I wasn't a preacher. I wasn't the leader of "that movement." I was just Caleb, the same boy who played Navy Seals with Nerf guns in the backyard. The innocent little kid who loved being with his grandfather. The boy who loved building blocks, Capri Sun, and adventure with his dad. The boy who repeatedly asked his fourth-grade teacher, "Am I doing this right?" (I've always needed affirmation.)

Mrs. Elise reminded me that my identity is simply being a child of God—loved, valued, and deeply cared for, never because of what I could do on my own, but simply because I am God's son . . . without anyone to impress, without critical opinions. Just Caleb.

God took those words and planted something deep down in my spirit that night.

Our identity is not in what we do, it's who we are. But I often wonder, do we even know who we are? Our culture loves to use our accomplishments as a placeholder for our identity. But these are shallow explanations of who we are. Our identity is so much deeper than what we have done or the title we may hold.

God sees much more in us. He doesn't want your achievements. He doesn't give you big dreams based on how well you're doing or how impressive you might become in the future. God just wants your heart! He knows you. You are His son or daughter. Stop trying to impress someone who knows you better than you know yourself.

Mrs. Elise reminded me that I wanted to be known for who I was, not for everything we're doing. Isn't that the truth for all of us? You've got your own things going in life, and you don't want to be known *only* for those accomplishments, right? At the end of the day, we want to be known. Intimately known. The good and the bad. The mistakes and the victories. We want to be known— and to truly feel that we are approved, trusted, loved.

I'm not The Alternative. Austin isn't The Alternative. If The Alternative crashes and burns tomorrow, it's not about me—I'm just Caleb. The same goes for you. Don't confuse your identity with what you do or who you know. Just because you're a doctor doesn't mean God sees you any differently than He sees an elementary school's custodian. Just because you're an athlete about to get a full-ride scholarship to college, that doesn't mean God is prouder of you than a kid who just got cut from the JV team. God's love for us is not dependent on or measured by our successes . . . or our failures. He loves us for who we really are.

> Don't confuse your identity with what you do or who you know.

Our culture tells us we should know our career plan while we are still in high school. Schools encourage us to go thousands of dollars into debt to get an education in the hope that we can land a career in a field we like when we're finished. Culture says we should know exactly what we want to do and what school we are going to attend. So, we jump into professions and majors in the hope we will find joy there, but we're missing the point.

The problem with mapping out our entire lives when we're young is we are still trying to figure out who we are, and we will never know what we are purposed to do—what really satisfies our soul—if we don't know who we are. I went to two colleges and changed my degree three times. I never finished. I got too distracted doing what I love, and now I get to do it every day. I have nothing against higher education, but I wouldn't change a thing about the way my life has played out—chasing dreams and living in hope.

Understanding who we are will help us step into our purpose. But discovering who we are takes courage. This journey of discovery is more about being vulnerable and accepting what God

It's all about passion and support.

is saying than it is just suddenly realizing who you are. That's why healthy, close community is so important. As you search for who God has made you to be, leaders and friends can speak into your life and affirm the great potential God has hidden in you, the way Mrs. Elise did for me.

It takes bravery to peel back the layers we have built up over the years—layers of defenses that hide our fear and failures. "Who am I?" might just be one of the most painful and difficult questions we all must answer if we really want to pursue the dream that God has set in our hearts. It's a question that leads us on a journey of discovery, searching our hearts for passion that is not tainted by others' opinions or pressures. You are not who your parents say you have to be. You are not who your friends want you to be. You are not what your failures say you are. But you are who God has destined and designed you to be. It is a passion fueled by the Holy Spirit and guided by His word, launching us into our divine purpose here on earth.

FAITHFUL IS ALL I NEED
THE PARABLE OF THE TALENTS

Do you remember the parable of the talents in Matthew 25? Jesus told this story, and it may be more applicable to our lives than we realize.

The man in the story is going on a journey, and he entrusts his wealth to three of his servants. One servant gets five bags, one servant gets three bags, and one servant gets one bag. The servant with five bags invested the money and made five more. The servant with two bags did the same and earned two more bags. But the servant who received one bag dug a hole, buried the gold, and left it there until his master returned.

When the master returned and saw what the one-bag servant had done, he was not pleased. The servant had hidden the gold in fear and had not used the resources that were entrusted to him. The master called him wicked and lazy. But when the master saw what each of his other two servants had done—that they'd taken what was given to them and increased it—he said, "Well done, good and faithful servant."

Let's just be clear here—this story isn't about money, necessarily, though of course we can and should be faithful with that resource. It wasn't about the specific amount of the return (notice one servant made more than twice what the other servant made, and the master's response to both was the same). The point of the story is that each had been entrusted with a particular amount, and the master expected them to use what they'd been given.

Do you notice what the master *didn't* say? He didn't say, "Well done, good and productive servant." Or, "Well done, good and popular servant . . . good and accomplished servant . . . good and pure servant." He said, "Well done, good and faithful servant."

See, this God of ours deeply values our attempts and our consistency, not our record of wins. What the servant with his one bag did was wicked and lazy because he didn't even attempt to use what he had for gain. He acted in fear and literally shoved what was given to him into a hole and left it there.

I don't know about you, but I'm tremendously relieved by the master's words. Here I am, spending my entire life striving, longing, and working toward great things. I want to be successful. I want to accomplish big things. I want to set records. I want to be known. I want to be loved. I want to do a lot. But is that really who God wants me to be? Is that my calling? I don't think it is, because God isn't going to see me any differently if I accomplish all those massive feats. God measures goodness by faithfulness, not by accolades.

According to the master's response, our performance on earth is rated not by how much we do, but by how faithful we are. When we think of this word *faithful*, we think of commitment and loyalty to a job or a person. That's a good definition, but perhaps the biggest challenge is to be faithful to *who* God created us to be, faithful to authenticity.

Not wavering. Not settling. Not giving in to the peer pressure around us. Not giving in to the temptation of short-term pleasure. Not allowing ourselves to shrink back to a place of comfort while God is calling us out. Not allowing ourselves to take the gifts and dreams and unique character traits that make us who we are and shove those things into a dark hole because we're afraid.

DO SOMETHING ABOUT IT

Have you ever been surprised when someone you looked up to knew you? Has someone you liked ever caught you off guard because they knew about you? They knew something special or intimate? That's the best! I remember meeting a longtime hero of mine once. Someone had obviously briefed him about who Austin and I were and what we'd been doing. I was caught off guard when my hero knew about me—shocked in a good way.

Those moments really leave an impact. It feels good to be known for something positive. And there's nothing wrong with celebrating those positives or being known for something good.

But once you understand that you are already loved and accepted by the God who knows your worst, your journey will take a dramatic shift. You are not working *for* approval. You're working *from* it. When you let that truth sink down deep, you will no longer spend your energy trying to gain everyone's acceptance. Rather, you'll live from a place of eternal approval: you're known by God!

He's watching what you do. You have His attention. If someone else disagrees with you, gets mad at you, lies about you . . . remember that God knows you, and that's all you need. Your identity is in who He is, after all. As you journey toward your purpose in this life, remember that God knows you and loves you, and that's who you are.

As a young communicator, I used to listen to the podcasts of a particular pastor all the time—while mowing the yard, driving down the road, working out. He was one of my favorite pastors and the only communicator I really listened to for an extended period of time.

As I consumed more and more of his words, I noticed that my own preaching ability was suffering because I was subconsciously morphing into a mini version of this pastor—illustrations, preaching style, all of it. My identity on the stage was becoming a duplicate of someone else. I was forgetting who I was and becoming someone I was never meant to be.

Whoops.

Many of us live like this: instead of embracing our own journey, we live in the shadow of someone else's dream. We don't have the courage to dream our own dreams, to preach our own messages, to make our own paths. We only wear what our friends wear—same shoes, same styles. We only pursue what our culture says is possible. We believe only to the limit that those around us believe.

Have you ever felt like this? Like you're not brave enough to be yourself yet, so you're trying to become someone you were never meant to be? Like every day that passes, you're slipping further and further from who you were meant to be? I don't think God is going to bless something He didn't create. He can't sustain something He hasn't destined. If you really want to see God bless your life, you have to embrace your own identity. Believe in what He has put in your heart. Don't copy people; just be you. Be confident. Be brave!

> If you really want to see God bless your life, you have to embrace your own identity.

God says that you are made in His image (Genesis 1:27). That means your smile, your joy, your laugh, your desire to love and to give, your ability to create and build, your compassion to forgive and love—these are all reflections of who God is in you.

Have you ever thought about the creation of *you*? Have you ever thought about the creation of the world? God could have made the world black and white, without color, but He didn't. He's creative, and you can trace your creativity back to Him. The same can be said of any passion you have.

If you really want to know yourself at the deepest level, you have to know God. If you really want to be secure, don't you need to be secure in Him? The more you walk with God, the better you'll understand yourself and the more your identity will become clear.

Psalm 139 says that you were knitted together in your mother's womb. Genesis talks about God creating the entire universe by the words He spoke and the breath He breathed. But when it came to you and me, when it came to the human heart, the Bible says that God knelt to the dirt and started working with His hands. Strategically, intentionally, carefully, He formed you and me by knitting us together.

I don't know about you, but knitting is not something I do. Props if that's you, but I'm not patient enough. Knitting well takes time and meticulous precision. That's how God made us. He didn't just speak us into existence. He didn't just think us into existence. He formed us.

You can have the biggest ministry, you can be the most popular athlete in the world, you can be the highest-paid actor or actress and still go home every night, lay your head on your pillow, and feel empty and unfulfilled because you haven't joined hands with the One who designed your soul and destined you to a life of purpose.

SELF-DISCOVERY LIST

Take a few minutes to think about what God says about you, things you know to be true about who He made you to be.

Now grab some paper. It's writing time. Start to write down these truths God has spoken to you. Without writing any of your accomplishments, titles, job positions, labels, accolades, or even failures. None of that is allowed here. Can you write about *who* you are?

Don't be afraid to be real and open and vulnerable here. You can be raw, even. This is God you're talking to. Your accomplishments don't impress Him as much as *you* impress Him. So, who are you, at your very core?

This may seem difficult, but that's okay. Reshape how you define your identity. Focus on those things about yourself you know to be true but maybe haven't fully embraced yet. That God loves you. That He created you with purpose. That you're accepted just the way you are. That you have specific value to bring to the world.

You're a reflection of your Creator.

JUST A SHADOW

BY PAUL HARRISON

Have you ever given much thought to your shadow? Honestly, neither have I until now. What does it say about us? One might say our shadows tell us we have form. Another might say that the shape it casts is unique because the image it bears is unique.

Now what does this say about our image in Christ? We are the silhouette or shadow of Christ. We are not Christ, but we are made in the image of Christ. Genesis 1:26–27 says, "Let us make mankind in our image . . . So God created mankind in his own image." Romans 8:29 states, "For those God foreknew he also predestined to be conformed to the image of his Son."

Now, what does any of this have to do with a shadow? If you think about it, your shadow is a type of reflection—it is not the full image of who you are.

This is the same as us when it comes to Christ. We are not Him, but we are to reflect Him to the world around us. We are representations of what is to come when Christ Himself returns. When we bear the image of Christ, we are also taking on His like-ness and attributes, also known as the "fruit of the spirit" found in Galatians 5:22–23. When people encounter the shadow of Christ in us, they are getting a small taste of who Christ is.

Being a shadow of Christ also means we imitate Christ and who He is. A shadow doesn't make any movement apart from the image that casts it. The same should be said of us. Do as Christ does; act as Christ acts. Right in the middle of washing the disciples' feet in John 13:12–17, He says, "I have set you an example that you should do as I have done for you."

This type of reflection in part means doing, but it also means being. We are part of a greater image. We are the bearer's reflection. Part of that means simply being His reflection. Yes, that includes doing, but it also means just being. We do not act on our own but in a manner that fully represents Christ.

Why do I tell you all this? Once we know whose image we bear, we are able to act and be accordingly. We are designed and created to glorify Christ and bear His image. A shadow silhouette is always attached to the image and does as the image does. To this end, stay attached to Christ, and do and be as Christ is and does.

CHAPTER 11

WHEN YOU KNOW, YOU KNOW

AUSTIN

I was sitting in a hotel ballroom, visiting a church that met there. When I say, "hotel ballroom," you might think this hotel was a Westin or Ritz Carlton. Nope, it was inside of a Days Inn in the middle of nowhere.

I was there only because my dad invited me to check out this church with him. I couldn't say no. I mean, it was my dad.

When we first walked in, I shook some hands but mostly kept to myself. I didn't know anyone, after all. My dad and I found a couple of seats. (You guessed it, front row—isn't that the way it always is when you're in a new place and you don't know any-one?) Worship was about to start, so we settled in.

I had no idea that what would happen next was going to change my life forever.

I was sixteen at the time, going through things that a lot of sixteen-year-olds go through. Dating, trying to fall in love, on the lookout for who I might marry. Yeah, these things were on my mind in those days, though maybe not right at that moment. At the time, I had also just stopped playing baseball—the sport I'd always dreamed of playing professionally. The team I was playing on had to make cuts, and after three years of playing for them, I was one of those sent home. I was asking God what was next for me. What was I supposed to do with my life now?

I think most of us have been there at one point or another, whether you're fifteen or fifty. Maybe you're there more often than not! We're always dreaming, searching for what next week will look like, what next year might bring, or where we hope to be in five or ten years.

That's where I was that day.

As worship began, I realized this wasn't just another church. The people in this room really *knew* what worship was. They connected deeply with who they were worshiping. You could see it. You could feel it.

I had never been around people worshiping so deeply before. Or people dancing to the worship music, or lying facedown on the ground, crying out to God. It was an entirely new church experience, and I was blown away.

The service had only been going for ten or fifteen minutes when the lady who was leading worship walked up to me and asked, "Are you Buddy's son?"

"Yes, ma'am," I replied.

"Can I pray for you?"

"Sure!" Of course, I had no idea what was about to happen. My enthusiasm in agreeing to let her pray for me must have been from the Holy Spirit—one of those moments where you let go for no good reason. I believe the Holy Spirit wanted to speak to me.

She began to pray then, speaking things over my life. Her prayer seemed to be drawing to a close, and then she looked right at me and said, "The girl you are in a relationship with now is not your wife."

Um, what did you just say?

How did she know I was in a relationship? And how did she know anything about my girlfriend?

She went on. "You will know your wife because she will have the breastplate of righteousness on. She will carry a sword in each hand, and you will see the love she has for God all over her."

I had to fight back tears. So many different thoughts swirled through my mind. Shock that she knew anything about my current relationship. Excitement about this woman she described—that girl sounded pretty amazing! And, also, a twinge of anger that my current girlfriend supposedly wasn't the right one.

I remember leaving that night, getting in the car, and remaining silent the whole car ride home—kind of in a state of wonder.

What was going to happen? How would this woman's words come true? *Would* they come true? Or was this just an out-there experience I should dismiss?

I made up my mind then. I decided if those statements were real and the girl I was in a relationship with wasn't my wife, God was going to have to clearly show me. I wasn't acting on the word of some woman I didn't even know. God would need to step in and make something happen.

So, I wrote down the words the woman had spoken to me, put them in a drawer, and promptly forgot about them. I didn't want to think about them. I definitely didn't want to act on them. So I didn't.

But, two months later, my relationship ended. It took another month for me to remember what had happened in the hotel ballroom, but then I started to wonder. Maybe those words really had been from God. Maybe she did know what she was talking about.

Four years later, in 2014, I still hadn't met my wife.

I was serving at a church in Newnan, helping lead a group and preaching at their Wednesday night gatherings for their high school ministry. I met a couple that was on staff at the time—the husband, Jeff, was the worship leader, and the wife, Jess, was a

The Man Monday group, and our friends at ThreeLife (including Rachel, front and second from left, and Jess and Jeff, front right).

leader within the high school ministry. They approached me one day, asking if I was interested in being part of a small group of people who hung out on Monday nights at their house.

This small group mainly consisted of me, Caleb, and our friend Tyler, but it sounded fun, so I went. We started calling it "Man Monday" (no judging). The three of us would grab food from the late-night menu at Smokey Bones and hang out. We did this for months. The group got pretty tight. It was community—true community—even if it was a small one. There was vulnerability in that group—the freedom to be open and imperfect. Those relationships were a pillar in my life.

Jeff and Jess would always ask us, "Are you dating anybody?"

And we would always answer, "No, Jess."

It was great. One Monday night, we were hanging out, getting ready for a big youth event on Wednesday. We were blowing up enough balloons to fill an entire room for a game with our high schoolers when Jess walked up to me.

"I found your wife," she said.

Automatically, I responded, "Yeah, right. Everyone says that to me."

"No, really."

I almost rolled my eyes. "Okay, show me a picture."

"No. I want you to meet her in person."

"Fine. When can I meet her?"

"Well, she doesn't live in Georgia. But she's moving to Newnan in the fall."

Now I did roll my eyes. It was June. "Okay, whatever. I'll meet her in three months."

Jess didn't say anything else about it, and after a while, I forgot she'd ever brought it up.

That August, Caleb and I were setting up for an Alternative event—getting the stage ready, putting out chairs, and all the typical things we do before any event.

My phone rang, and I checked the caller ID. It was Jess. "Hey, Jess."

"Hey, Jeff and I are at Chick-fil-A. What do you want to eat?"

I relayed our orders and then went back to work.

After a while, the door opened. It was Jeff and Jess with our food, but someone else was with them too. Jeff and Jess handed Caleb his food, and this mystery person handed me mine.

Then Jess said, nice and casual, "Oh, Austin, this is Rachel—my friend who is moving here from Alabama."

Ah-ha. Jess's plan became obvious in about two seconds.

I smiled at Rachel. "Hey, I'm Austin. Nice to meet you. Thanks for the food."

She smiled back. "You're welcome."

Then we both fell silent, because you can imagine how awkward this was. So that was it. For the time being, at least.

A few months passed, and Rachel moved to Newnan, as planned. She started hanging with our group, and we all became good friends. But . . . we weren't interested in each other romantically. She was attractive. Obviously. But I wasn't thinking, "I need to date this girl!" We were just great friends.

One Monday night while we were having dinner together, Jeff and Jess informed us they were going to take another job at a church in north Atlanta. They asked if we would fast with them for the next week while we prayed about their transition.

We were excited for them, pumped to be a part of what was next for them and their family. But then they added, "We don't want you guys to just fast about what our future looks like, but what *yours* will look like too."

I'm the type of person who always wants to know what's next, and that was certainly true in this moment. I was ready to do some great things—to take steps that would challenge me. So, this seemed like a good time to write down goals for the upcoming year, 2015.

The list was long. I wanted to get married. I wanted to work full time at a church. I wanted to preach at lots of different places. The list went on and on.

Three days into the fast, Tyler and I were driving through town, talking about life, and he asked me the most random question: "Would you be okay with Rachel dating someone else?"

"No," I said immediately. Then I sat there in shock—shock at his question and shock at my answer.

My eyes slowly began to open. She'd been sitting there, right in front of me for months.

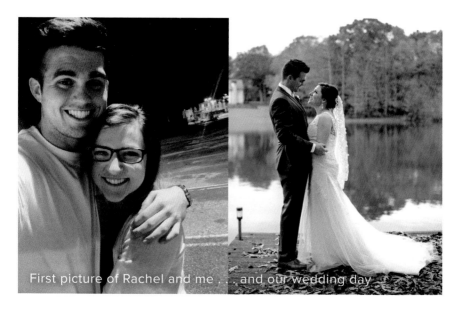

First picture of Rachel and me . . . and our wedding day

My wife. Whoa.

How had I not seen it before? She carried herself with such confidence, knowing her worth as a child of God. She was nurturing and kind, and I could absolutely see myself pursuing her for marriage.

A month later, we went on our first date. Three months later, we were engaged. Four months after that, we were married—eight months to the day after our first date.

RUTH AND BOAZ
BOOK OF RUTH

When my wife and I first began to "talk," or however you'd phrase it, she kind of played hard to get. But, really, she just wanted me to pursue her. She wouldn't even text me first, so I was left looking for excuses to text her. (I ended up going with shoes—you know, texting different pairs to her, asking her opinion. Because that's what people text about, right? But, hey, it worked.)

When you think about it, we all want to be pursued. What we might not realize is that we *are* being pursued, no matter what our current romantic status is. Let me explain.

The story of Ruth and Boaz gives us a pretty clear picture of this. In the beginning of the book of Ruth, we learn that Ruth was a Moabite married to an Israelite man and living in Moab. Ruth's Israelite husband passed away, and she decided to stay with her mother-in-law, Naomi, as Naomi traveled back to Israel. It would have been normal for a widow to go back and live with her birth family, but Ruth insisted that wherever her mother-in-law went, she would go, and Naomi's people would become her people (Ruth 1:16).

So Ruth went to live with Naomi's people, even though it meant going out in the field and working to support their new household. She eventually made her way to Boaz's field. Intrigued by the newcomer, he asked about her.

Boaz then sought Ruth out and told her that she did not need to go work anywhere else. She could stay there instead, drink the water that he provided, and stay close to the servants that were there. By this small gesture, Boaz was taking Ruth in and treating her like she was one of his own people, when she was actually a foreigner. When it came time for them to eat, Boaz offered her bread and wine, and the remaining leftovers, to take back to her mother-in-law as well.

Ruth went back that night and began to tell Naomi about the man she was working for. Naomi was filled with excitement for her daughter-in-law. She knew Boaz was a man after God's heart and would treat Ruth how she should be treated. After some time had passed, Naomi asked Ruth if she'd like for her to build a house for Ruth so that she could live a happy life. This was basically code for "Hey, Ruth—do you want to go out and meet someone? Get remarried? Start a family?" The talk came up again about Boaz, and Naomi sent Ruth to one of Boaz's parties so they could connect again.

In this culture, however, a widow needing to remarry was supposed to go to the "next closest" relative in line to be married back into the family. That may seem like a weird practice to our culture, but stay with me here. While Boaz was related to Ruth's husband who had passed away, there was someone closer in line who had marriage rights. Boaz followed the law and notified the closer relative, but he also went out of his way to pursue Ruth. He paid a very high price—purchasing Naomi's husband's land, which was a huge deal during this time.

Ruth and Boaz got married and had children. King David was their descendant.

The story of Ruth and Boaz is one of pursuit and sacrifice—one that we try to mimic in our relationships. However, even more than that, it is a picture of how Jesus pursues us, offers the best He has, and paid the ultimate sacrifice because He loves us. Ruth and Boaz give us a great example of godly pursuit to follow in our romantic relationships. But let's not miss the bigger lesson here: no matter what's happening in your love life, God pursues each of us like Boaz pursued Ruth—with love, protection, care, and sacrifice.

DO SOMETHING ABOUT IT

A few months after Rachel and I got married, I ran into the lady from the hotel ballroom church. Seriously. I hadn't seen or spoken to her for five years, and out of the blue, I got a knock on my office door while I was working in LaGrange. It was her. Her name is Michelle.

"Hi, Austin! How are you doing?" Michelle asked.

"Well," I said, "I got married a few months ago."

She grinned. "How exciting! What's her name?"

"Rachel."

Michelle froze for a second, and then her smile grew bigger. "Do you remember back in 2010 when I spoke over your life?"

How could I forget? "Yes, ma'am."

"That night, I went home and wrote your wife's name in my journal. I have it still—on a note somewhere in my journal. Rachel."

I didn't try to fight the tears that time. I couldn't believe it. Except, of course, I did believe it, because that's the way God works. He is so faithful to His word—then, now, and always.

As I write this, Rachel and I have been married almost three years. We have a sixteen-month-old baby girl. God has been very good.

Getting married young isn't the easiest thing in the world. But my marriage is one of the most rewarding things I've ever been part of. Sometimes we miss the real heart of marriage in our culture. We think of it as a legal agreement, and it's that too, but even more so, it's a covenant—a binding promise between husband, wife, and God.

As a man, my roles have changed drastically since 2010 when I was that sixteen-year-old sitting in a hotel ballroom. Getting married carries with it a huge responsibility. My wife and I are supposed to love each other sacrificially. We're supposed to care deeply about each other's needs. After God, she is my first priority.

That's a huge calling for both of us. I'm accountable to God for my whole family now, not just myself. Rachel and our little girl, Esther, depend on me to protect them. Someday, maybe Esther will marry, and her husband will take over that role.

Which I will allow when she's sixty years old, so we're good for a while.

But seriously. Think about that: being married is a massive responsibility. It's serious. It's weighty. It has significance in this life and in eternity. Marriage and parenthood are not roles to be taken lightly. That's why we treat the marriage relationship as sacred. We honor God in our dating lives as a reflection of that too.

I'm not going to lie. I don't know a ton about marriage. I'm still pretty new at it. And I bet even after being married for twenty years, most people would say they're still learning.

Though I don't know a lot about marriage, I do know how to

love and serve my wife. I do understand my responsibility to her, and I appreciate the role she plays in my world too. The serving, love, and sacrifice between husband and wife definitely goes both ways.

You may ask why I gave so many personal details in this chapter (some might even call it oversharing!). It's because I wanted to show you the faithfulness of God throughout my life. I'm not perfect as a husband or a father, and I'm still learning to lead my wife and daughter every day. But God proves Himself to be faithful on this journey over and over. He knew Rachel was going to be my wife, and He knew Esther was going to be my daughter.

He knows His plan for my life, and He equips me to live it day by day.

I know the story of how Rachel and I ended up together is pretty crazy. Prophetic words aren't usually part of the equation when it comes to picking our spouses, and I get that. But there are some universal truths in my story that you can apply to your dating life, no matter what your details may look like.

First, be open to the things that people you love and respect speak into your life. Sure, my example is a little wild. Michelle was a stranger, and she was speaking over my life in a particular way. But I bet your parents, pastors, mentors, teachers, leaders, and others who are close to you have spoken wisdom, strength, and good things into your life for as long as they've known you. Hold on to those things. While it's important that we find our own way and not live for others' expectations when it comes to choosing a partner, it's also important to balance that independence with a willingness to listen to those who may have lived a little more life than we have.

Second, we need to keep in focus the things that matter to God when we're choosing a partner. Marriage is no joke. We're talking about the rest of our lives. So, do you really want to focus on the things the world says are important—good looks, money, success, or talent? Or do you want to focus on the things God values—faithfulness, kindness, goodness, and spiritual maturity?

Focus on the things God focuses on. Put those priorities first, and it'll serve you well.

I'm not going to lie. My wife is gorgeous. There's nothing wrong with physical attractiveness, success in your life, or being blessed with money. But what caused me to fall in love with her was her heart. It was the breastplate of righteousness, those swords of truth in her hands, and the love she has for God all over her, just like Michelle said. Focus on the things God focuses on. Put those priorities first, and it'll serve you well in your search for "the one."

I know this chapter is about dating and marriage, but these truths apply to other relationships too. Sometimes we don't take the selection of our friends as seriously as we should. The people you surround yourself with help determine the direction of your life. The Bible phrases it a little differently than that, but the truth still stands. Be intentional about the friendships you choose to invest in. Surround yourself with people you respect and who respect you. Look for qualities in those friends that are God-honoring. Friendships like these build you (and your friend!) up and help keep you on the path God wants you to pursue.

TREASURED RELATIONSHIPS

Take a minute to jot down the names of the people you appreciate most in your life. Maybe that's your significant other, your parents, extended family, friends, mentors, teachers, or coaches.

Select a handful of names from this list of awesome people who have poured love and support into your life. Now spend about ten or fifteen minutes writing a card, sending an email, or even just shooting them a text. Let them know how much you care about them. Tell them why their support has meant so much to you.

This might not be something you'd typically do (am I right, guys?), but it's only ten or fifteen minutes for each of the people who have mattered most to you. You can do this. Maybe even include one thing you plan to do to help them know how valued they are—how much you appreciate all their love and support.

Maybe start with three people, but keep going if you want. It never hurts to tell people they matter to us. It never hurts to make sure our loved ones know that we care, and that their care of us hasn't gone unnoticed.

I don't know anyone who regrets expressing their love and says, "I wish I had not told them as often how much I loved them." Do you?

SMALL HURTS, BIG PROBLEMS

BY JEFFERSON BETHKE

My wife Alyssa and I were both sitting on the couch one evening. I remember her asking me nicely to go get something she needed from the bedroom. Being selfish and tired and grumpy that night, I said, "Why don't you go get it?" or something to that effect. (I have a feeling I'm not the only one who's done this.)

That comment quickly escalated into both of us being upset, grumpy, and rude to each other. I later apologized and felt so dumb because it was the tiniest thing she'd asked for—and yet, my reaction was not the tiniest thing.

And that was when a phrase from some of our married friends came into my head. A few weeks prior, we were at dinner talking about marriage advice. I remember them saying one of the best pieces of advice they got was, "Bring up little things in a little way, and big things in a big way." It's simple, but sadly overlooked. Looking back on my relationship with Alyssa, so many petty arguments or breakdowns in communication have happened because our frustration wasn't proportional to the actual issue at hand.

And so Alyssa and I have made a commitment to that principle. And it's made all the difference. It gives us an excuse to bring up the little things in a little way *before* they turn out to be big things. Because a lot of times, something small will hurt our feelings or upset us, and in our minds we say, "Oh, that's no big deal. I need to get over it." But if those things remain unsaid, the small hurts start to add up and eventually create a disproportional response that makes things worse. Instead, Alyssa and I have committed to saying in the little things, "Hey, that little comment hurt me."

Or, "Not a huge deal, but I just wanted to let you know, I feel overlooked today."

Or, "When I asked you to do something, it means a lot when you do, especially after a long day taking care of the kids."

It's a subtle shift, but it's one that saves you from a lot of unnecessary heartache and frustration, and one that also brings in grace in a beautiful way—extending the benefit of the doubt, seeing the other person how Jesus sees them, and acting in love.

CHAPTER 12

ALWAYS ENOUGH

AUSTIN

Five years ago, if you had told me God would choose two guys out of the small town of Newnan, Georgia, to do anything big for Him, I wouldn't have believed you. Two guys who were messed up and running from the dream God had put on their hearts—a dream to be part of a Jesus generation who would not just leave a small mark on history but who would *make* history.

I should have believed, though. I should have believed because God had been planning it for a long time. Before I had any idea what kind of ministry I might work with or how I might change the world for God, a church had taken up an offering for me. Well, not for *me*, exactly, but for my dream. I had mentioned that I really wanted to do something for the kingdom. Even though I was a teenager, and I had no clue what I wanted to do, this church believed in me.

Their offering for my future ministry totaled over six hundred dollars. I was blown away by that generosity. I had no idea what to do with all that money, since I didn't actually have a ministry yet. But it was a sign that my community believed in the calling on

Only God could have done this—2012 versus a gathering in 2017.

my life. I put the money aside for safekeeping and knew I would do something with it for the kingdom someday.

Years later, while I was still in high school, some friends and I decided to use some of that ministry money to purchase a bunch of camouflage-print Bibles. (Hey, we were just ordinary rednecks having bonfires on the weekends.) We figured passing out those Bibles at East Coweta High School would do some good and reach people for Christ. Even then, while we handed out those Bibles, we were dreaming about the day when thousands would worship together in this city.

And that happened. Newnan, Georgia, has never seen a move of God like we're seeing right now. But you know what? God's idea was even bigger than what my friends and I had dreamed at that time. I never imagined we would share the gospel all over the country.

Every month we have groups and individuals fly in from all over the country. Virginia, Texas, California, Arkansas, Minnesota, Florida, the Carolinas—we've even gone international and had people from Canada and Australia come to be a part of what is happening in our community.

We all want to be used by God. But if we are truthful, a lot of us don't make it to that point because of the failures and mistakes we have made and experienced. As I look back on some of the biggest movements and game-changing moments in history, I see that the individuals God used were just a bunch of ordinary people. Not people who have a perfect portfolio, the best record, the biggest bank account, the prettiest family, the nicest home, or even the best actions. God has always been in the business of using people who are good at screwing it all up—the people others have disqualified.

EVEN PETER DENIED
JOHN 18

If you've ever felt like you are too much of a screwup to be used by God, let me tell you a story to encourage you. Peter was one of the first disciples called by Jesus. He was a professional fisherman, and his faith was so firm that Jesus gave him the name *Cephas*, which means "rock" in Aramaic. He was an ordinary guy, but he had a lot going for him. All he had to do was walk straight. Instead, he messed it all up.

Jesus was in the final part of his ministry on earth. It was about time for him to go to the cross. Jesus was seized and tied up by the temple guards, and they took him to Caiaphas. Caiaphas was the high priest that year, and it was Caiaphas who wanted Jesus dead.

In the high priest's courtyard, a young woman who was with the doorkeeper asked Peter if he was one of Jesus's disciples.

Here was Peter's chance to stand up for the truth!

But instead he said, "No, I'm not."

Jesus was inside being interrogated and beaten. Peter was huddled around the fire outside, and again someone asked him, "Aren't you one of His disciples?"

He denied it. "Not me."

And then, once again, a servant asked, "Didn't I see you in the garden with Him?"

Third time's the charm? Not so much. Peter denied Christ *again*.

Now, since I said this story was supposed to encourage you, let's talk about what happened in the rest of Peter's life. He realized he'd denied his Lord. He repented, and Jesus fully forgave him. He was back to Peter, the rock. Peter, the believer. And in his ministry after Jesus ascended to heaven, Peter was bold, strong, and effective. He did far more than he'd done in the earlier part of his ministry.

Peter's capacity to screw things up didn't change his identity or the calling on his life. God still used him mightily. And no matter where we come from or how we've failed in the past, God can use us too.

DO SOMETHING ABOUT IT

Don't you love how God has used real people throughout history to accomplish His work? Ordinary people with extraordinary stories.

By the time Peter's big screwup took place, he had already accomplished great things at Jesus's side. And yet, at the moment when fear and uncertainty were highest, he let Jesus down. Peter realized in this moment that if he claimed he was a disciple of Jesus, he would likely be executed—and he gave in to that fear.

It's easy for us to judge him in hindsight, but think about his position for a minute. Have you ever been in a situation where you felt pretty sure you'd lose your life if you stood up for your faith? Most of us haven't.

But we *have* been in situations where we've been given the opportunity to stand up for something that may be unpopular but that we know is right—to stand out and go against the grain in a way that's scary. We might lose friends. We might get mocked or rejected.

How often have we played it safe in those situations? How often have we denied the desire to be different? Whether it's in front of family, friends, or a girlfriend or boyfriend, it can be terrifying to stand up and speak out.

We should be bold enough to stand out, to speak up, but we often choose to go with the flow, and the cost is often compromise. Compromise of our core selves. Compromise of our faith.

Without boldness, we won't grasp the dreams we've been talking about.

I don't mean to be harsh, but we live in a time when people talk a lot about chasing their dreams—we're the dreamer generation. It's great to be called a dreamer, but if a person only dreams and never acts on that dream, what is the point of having it? Those dreams sit unused in our minds, collecting dust.

Maybe you want to own your own business one day, but you are currently looking at what it will cost you. I'm not only talking financially, but physically. Maybe it would mean downsizing, selling a vehicle so you'd have enough capital to start your business. Maybe it would mean late nights, stress, or stepping away from the position you currently hold at your job. Or maybe you realize you are in a relationship that is toxic; you recognize you need to remove yourself from the situation, but the cost of what people might think is holding you back.

For some people, the fear runs even deeper. Maybe it stems from a serious hurt that has made it difficult to even dare to think of the dream God has placed in your heart. Because when we've been let down over and over by our own failures or the failures of others, sometimes we think it's not even worth trying anymore.

I think Jesus and Peter may have both felt like it wasn't worth trying anymore during the moments surrounding Peter's denial—Jesus when He knew His friend had turned his back on Him, and Peter when he realized the depth of his betrayal.

The only way I can try to understand what Jesus must have felt is to compare Peter's betrayal to how I would feel if my own daughter were to deny me. It would break my heart. It would crush me. Fear can cloud us to the point that we cause this kind of hurt to the people we love most, as Peter did.

Peter was living in fear, not faith.

Fear doesn't come from God—it comes from Satan. Fear gives Satan power and control in our lives. Faith invites God into the picture. Being courageous is rarely convenient.

And we fail.

Sometimes people walk away from everything when they fail. They walk away from their dreams, their goals, even their faith. But our failures don't disturb God the way they disturb us. God didn't choose you because of your performance. He chose you because of your purpose. No matter how many times we mess up, He still says we're loved, and He still has a plan for us.

> Being courageous is rarely convenient.

Peter was shown grace. We are shown grace. Peter's story and countless others like it show us a deep, wonderful truth—the mistakes of the past do not dictate your future!

If you've ever felt like your mistakes disqualify you, hear what I'm saying right now: your sin is not enough to surpass the grace of God. God trumps every failure and mistake you have made. Don't give up hope. Don't use failure as an excuse to let your calling collect dust. God gave you a dream. He equipped you with vision and a calling. He gave you tools and passion and community. You—just you—are enough to do all God is asking of you.

Get after it.

Dream big, and hold nothing back.

REFLECTING

I think this is the perfect time to stop and reflect on how this book has affected you. Maybe it has helped awaken a dream that has been dead for a long time. Maybe it has given you ideas to unite your community. Maybe it has given you hope—hope that you still have a chance to make a huge impact in this world.

It's time to take those ideas and turn them into reality. Take that dream that's been a sentence written in your journal or has been stuck to the wall in your room on a sticky note, and make it happen. What is one thing you can do—one action, however small—to help get closer to that dream? Maybe your dream is to start a ministry. Take a step by writing a mission statement. Maybe your dream is to start a business. Right now, brainstorm ten ways to raise some capital. Maybe your dream is to write a book. Sit down, and write the first page.

Go for it. Take the leap. Don't spend another day looking at your life and questioning whether you have value in this world— know that you already do. With Jesus, we have everything we need. No matter the mistakes we've made or the dreams we've failed to realize so far, with Jesus we have what it takes. Rather than letting this truth make us complacent, let's use it to give us the confidence to *take action*.

Awaken that dream, and walk in hope.

MORE THAN ENOUGH

BY TONY NOLAN

She looked like a raccoon. Her mascara was so smeared from tears that I couldn't help but smile. However, what she was asking me was no laughing matter. She wanted to know how I made it, how I had overcome the fallout and emotional trauma of abuse. How had I been able to move on and stand in front of millions of people and tell my story? The cuts on her wrist revealed she wasn't just a curious millennial. She was desperate.

I've not walked in her shoes, but I have crawled many miles on her street. I was born in a mental institution. My biological mom was disturbed. I was beaten, molested, and tortured by foster care predators. My alcoholic adoptive dad repeatedly beat me and would scream that he regretted "buying" me. Seeking relief, I became addicted to narcotics and alcohol. I wrestled with suicidal thoughts and ended up in a mental ward like my mom. That's why the smudged-face, scarred-arm girl was reaching out to me. We had both tallied up a massive number of frequent crawler miles.

She waited for my response. I whispered one word to her . . . *Jesus.* She blinked and pushed a tear off the edge of her eyelid. It morphed from clear to black as it streaked through her makeup and down her trembling cheek. With a broken voice, she said, "I so need Him." We prayed. God answered. And her life was transformed from crawler to soarer, just like mine. Rescue is so beautiful.

You may read this and think, "It's not that simple." You're right. It's not; it's messy and complicated on so many exhausting levels. However, Jesus is that powerful. It's not simple, but no one can deny that the name of Jesus carries with it the power to cripple demons and, at the same time, to lift crawlers out of darkness.

Jesus is more than enough.

Hurting people are divided by racial barriers, political walls, and gender barricades. I still believe Jesus is their answer. Theoretically and theologically, you do too. However, in the heated battles of our culture, sometimes we act as retaliators instead of rescuers.

A story about the Berlin Wall can reorient our posture. The east side of the wall was the Soviet-occupied sector, and the west was a haven for freedom. One day, the Soviets dumped a massive pile of raw sewage and rotten garbage over the wall onto the guardhouse on the west side. The western guards were furious and wanted to retaliate. But their captain calmed them down and promised they could counter in the darkness of night. And counter they did! At sunrise, the Soviet soldiers came out of their guardhouse and found a neatly stacked twelve-foot-high pyramid of non-perishable goods: bottled water, cans of beans, bags of sugar, sacks of wheat, tobacco, blankets, clothing, and boots. On top of the goods was a small note that read, "Each side gives what each side has to give."

This story may or may not be true, but the lesson still applies. Some people give us grief because it's all they've got. But we have Jesus! I pray this book has birthed within your heart a renewed confidence in Jesus—confidence so strong that you can wipe off the garbage others have dumped on you and give them Jesus in return. In so doing, both the crawlers and the soarers, and everyone in between, discover that Jesus is more than enough. As we know, that Berlin Wall isn't there anymore. We have an alternative to walls: *Jesus.*

CONCLUSION

You've heard some of our story—the ups and downs, the good, the bad. We've talked about remembering God's promises and how God is always faithful. We've talked about moving past the mistakes of yesterday and embracing the future God has for you. We've challenged you as we've been challenged—to try again, to not give up.

But we want to leave you with one last thought: people are waiting on you.

They may not know it yet. They may not realize that your dream—the very thing God has called you to do—might just free them. It might be the thing that moves them, inspires them, encourages them, or challenges them. They don't know it yet, but they're waiting on you. God has allowed us to be part of His redemption story by bringing hope to those around us.

We want to challenge you right now. Don't just accept our stories as mere inspiration. Don't read them, feel moved for a moment, and then forget about them.

Act.

We're praying you will. We're praying you will act on what God has called you to. Listen to His voice. Be obedient to His call. The world is waiting for you to get uncomfortable. Dreams will cost you comfort, but being uncomfortable breeds courage, and courage will invite others into your story. So, go for it. Dream big, build community, and share hope. Create your path.

The world needs your story.

—Austin and Caleb

ACKNOWLEDGMENTS

CALEB

I can remember looking at my teacher, asking, "Is this okay? Am I doing this right?" All I really wanted was someone to tell me I was doing a good job, to cheer me on and believe in me. I wouldn't be here today without the voice of my parents, who didn't just cheer me on, they told me when I was being stupid, and they placed me around the right people. They showed me what love looked like.

Luke Ayers, you practically bought stock in Waffle House with all of our late-night talks. You taught me what it looked like to live differently, to be passionate, to do hard things. Thank you.

Thanks to my brothers, Joshua and Nathan, who keep things fun when I get too busy. Life isn't perfect, but embrace what you have. I am always in your corner. Love you two.

Thanks to my grandfather, Allan, for showing me how to live a life of adventure, sip black coffee like it's water, and tell stories like our lives depended on it. You set a standard for our entire family to love vulnerably, speak intentionally, and champion people even when they are different. Our ministry would look a lot different if you didn't bring all those kids to our first events. I wish more people could have seen how passionate you were about reaching people with the gospel. I'm following that. You believed in me more than I ever did, and that gave me the courage I needed to keep going; still does. Thanks for the memories and all the love … see you soon.

At the end of the day, I want those closest to me to know how much I appreciate what they have given me. I couldn't be here without the countless hours served at Alternative gatherings, the speakers carried, the trusses lifted, the money donated, the things people will never know or see. To the Alternative Family, thank you for believing in something bigger than yourself, for embracing dreams, uniting communities carrying hope to those who need it most. Our most exciting moments are still ahead of us. Remember, keep the main thing the main thing and don't miss an opportunity.

AUSTIN

ONLY GOD. This opportunity would not have been possible without the provision God has had on my life. Writing this book has taught me so much on how to overcome our fears and insecurities. For years, writing has terrified me, so I never wrote. I was so insecure about the words I was jotting down in a Word document, thinking they were stupid, that the message I was trying to convey was going to sound dumb to people and they would never enjoy reading my content. But thank God for surrounding me with people who encouraged the heck out of me to just got for it.

To my family: my wife, Rachel, and daughter, Esther; my mother and father, Dina and Buddy; my sister, Amanda; and my grandmother (Mewmaw), thank you for supporting this project from the beginning. Thank you to the people who have walked life with me in years past who have helped strengthen my character for moments like these. And to the leaders in my life who have discipled me, challenging my faith and pushing my focus to Jesus, thank you.

To my friends who are brothers to me: Matt Morris, Luke Lezon, Jordan King. What a crew you guys are. I thank God for bringing you guys into my life.

To Michelle Rogers: thank you for prophesying over my life in 2010; that a movement would be born and that it would impact the whole world–speechless.

Finally, to one of my best friends, Caleb Stanley. What an honor, let's keep stepping.

CONTRIBUTOR BIOGRAPHIES

JORDAN KING

Jordan King was a member of the same youth group as Caleb Stanley and Austin Dennis. After attending Hillsong College in Sydney, Australia, Jordan felt called to come back to the city he grew up in and be a part of The Alternative. Today, Jordan helps lead worship and write songs for The Alternative. He represents The Alternative at several camps and events around the southeast. Jordan and his wife, Katie, both live in Newnan, Georgia.

NIGEL WALLACE

Nigel moved to Atlanta in 2017 after flying in for several Alternative gatherings. *Unorthodox* is the one word that best describes Nigel. Daily, his heart for seeing change within the world meets his creativity. Eternally inspired, Nigel uses the mediums of music, visual art, and poetry to express the perspectives and messages God lays on his heart. Early on, Nigel focused on using his powerful spoken words, but now helps create moments that include all mediums of creativity for The Alternative, his church, and the growing platform God continues to give him.

BRIAN PRESTON

Brian Preston is a builder. He started off building tables, but now he helps build futures for other men. As an article by CNN stated, "Not only producing expertly crafted furniture, he's restoring hope." It all started when Brian began a small furniture shop, employing underprivileged men who needed a job. Brian's company, Lamon Luther, has since exploded with growth, bringing products and hope to people all across the country.

MASEY MCLAIN

Masey McLain is an actress best known for her role as Rachel Joy Scott in the film *I'm Not Ashamed*. Since a young age, Masey has felt called to professionally act, and signed with an agency in Atlanta following a commercial with the Jonas Brothers. Today, Masey continues to pursue her calling as an actress while leveraging avenues such as speaking and writing to influence others to make a difference with their lives. Masey is the author of a devotional entitled *It's Worth It*, and currently plays Ashley Baxter on the new MGM/Roma Downey TV series *The Baxters*—a scripted drama based on the book series by Karen Kingsbury.

LUKE LEZON

Luke Lezon grew up in Dallas, Texas, before graduating from Texas A&M University with a degree in Communications, minoring in Creative Studies. After graduating, Luke married his wife, Lindsey, and co-planted Hill City Church in Fayetteville, Arkansas. After pastoring at Hill City for two years, Luke and his wife moved to and currently live in Atlanta, Georgia, where they help lead The

Alternative. Luke is a creative, dynamic preacher and teacher of God's Word with a palpable love for people.

GRANT SKELDON

Grant Skeldon started Initiative Network with the intention of shifting the culture of Dallas by training millennials to be Christ-loving, city-changing, church-investing, disciple-making local missionaries. Initiative Network has impacted thousands of young leaders from over 540 different churches across the metro-plex. Grant has also traveled the world, speaking to over 40,000 pastors, parents, and business leaders on the topic of engaging and empowering millennials. Grant is the author of *The Passion Generation*, published by Zondervan.

ADAM WEBER

Adam Weber is the lead pastor of Embrace Church, which over ten years has grown to six campuses and four thousand+ people in weekly attendance, and continues to grow. In 2013, 2014, and 2015, Embrace was listed as one of the fastest-growing churches in America according to *Outreach Magazine*. Adam is also the author of the bestselling book *Talking with God*, and is married to his beautiful wife, Becky. Together they have four kids: Hudson, Wilson, Grayson, and Anderson.

JOSH RHYE

After watching his father miraculously survive cancer and then losing his brother to suicide, Josh Rhye and his wife, Amanda, started ThreeLife Church south of Atlanta, Georgia. They began with thirteen people in a little cabin by a lake, and since 2013 have seen hundreds come to know Jesus and thousands reached with the gospel.

CHELSEA CROCKETT

Chelsea Crocket made her debut on YouTube as BeautyLiciousInsider in 2011. Since, she has become an inspiration for millions of teens around the globe. Her channel includes makeup tutorials, advice about dating and relationships, and messages about her faith and her own journey. Chelsea has appeared on *TODAY* as well as in *Seventeen*, *Teen Vogue*, and *Trend Magazine*, among others. Her website, ChelseaCrockett.com, is home to thousands of beauty, fashion, lifestyle, and advice posts.

PAUL HARRISON

Paul Harrison lives in Atlanta, Georgia, and has served alongside The Alternative each month since January 2017. He is passionate about discipleship and loves to challenge the way others approach God's Word.

JEFFERSON BETHKE

Jefferson Bethke is the *New York Times* bestselling author of *Jesus > Religion* and *It's Not What You Think*. Jeff burst into the Christian conversation when his YouTube video "Why I Hate Religion But Love Jesus" received over seven million views within the first forty-eight hours. He and his wife, Alyssa, are both authors and YouTube personalities who influence millions around the world. Jeff and his wife live in Maui with their daughter, Kinsley, and son, Kannon.

TONY NOLAN

Tony Nolan is passionate about communicating the gospel to those who are hurting and broken, and his ministry transforms hundreds of thousands of people every year. Tony has communicated the gospel with evangelical groups at Casting Crowns concerts, the LifeSong tour, Winter Jam, and hundreds of other events and festivals around the world. Tony is the author of several books, including *Hurt Healer: Reaching Out to a Broken World* and *GASP! You Will Spend Forever Somewhere: How to Make Sure It's Heaven.*

THE ALTERNATIVE

The Alternative is about thinking differently. Doing differently. Taking less-traveled roads. Creating your own path. Taking paths of great resistance. And actually making a difference in the lives around us . . . and the world at large.

If you're interested in joining our mission, or looking for more information on who we are and what we do, go to thealternative. org. There, you'll find the latest news on live events, volunteer opportunities, and what we're planning next.

And if you're hosting an event and would like to have The Alternative Band play, or want Austin or Caleb to speak to your group, email info@thealternative.org.

You can also follow us on social media:

 @TheAlternativee

 thealternativee

 thealternativeministries